The Myth of Tithing
and the Joy of Grace Giving

Shawn Lazar

Longview, TX

The Myth of Tithing and the Joy of Grace Giving @ 2024 by Shawn Lazar

Published by Free Grace International
2 Circle Rd
Longview, TX 75602
www.freegrace.in

Shawn Lazar (1978–)

ISBN: 978-1-68543-022-1 (Paperback)
978-1-68543-023-8 (Kindle)

Unless otherwise noted, all Scripture quotations from The Christian Standard Bible. Copyright © 2017 by Holman Bible Publishers. Used by permission.

All rights reserved. Any part of this publication may be reproduced, stored in a retrieval system, or transmitted in any form or by any means—electronic, mechanical, photocopy, recording or any other. The author gives permission to distribute this work freely, so long as it is not sold, and the wording is not changed.

Contents

Introduction 5
1. The Myth Examined 9
2. Christians Are Not Under Law 17
3. Principles of Grace Giving 33
4. Giving and the Heart 47
5. Trust God With Your Finances 59
Conclusion 69
Discussion Questions 71
Subject Index 77
Scripture Index 79
For Further Study 81

Introduction

"My heart breaks because much of the body of Christ is living under a curse," the preacher thundered. "That curse is a direct result of *stealing from God*."

Stealing from God? The congregation grew silent as the preacher began to read from Malachi 3.

"The truth of this passage seems so simple to me. If I tithe, I'm *blessed*. If I don't, I'm *cursed*. Hmmm, that's a tough decision," he mocked. "Let me think about that. Blessings or curses? Which do you want? For me, that one isn't that hard to figure out."

I want to be blessed, everyone thought.

The preacher stopped, was silent for a moment, and looked intently at the congregation. "If you don't tithe, that's an open door *to demons*."

I don't want a demon! The people squirmed, and you could hear the sounds of purses and wallets opening.

Have you ever suffered through a threatening sermon on giving?

Has a preacher accused you of *robbing* God because you don't *tithe*?

Has anyone ever threatened you with a *curse* if you don't give right then?

You might have felt scared or guilty. You may have written a check to avoid spiritual trouble. After all, why take the chance of being cursed by God or demons or both?

Christendom is full of fear-based messages about giving. They aim to make you open your wallet. The passage most often used comes from Malachi 3, where the prophet had some strong words for Israel. Let's read the whole passage before breaking it down:

> "Since the days of your ancestors, you have turned from my statutes; you have not kept them. Return to me, and I will return to you," says the Lord of Armies.
> Yet you ask, "How can we return?"
> "Will a man rob God? Yet you are robbing me!"
> "How do we rob you?" you ask.
> "By not making the payments of the tenth and the contributions. You are suffering under a curse, yet you—the whole nation—are still robbing me. Bring the full tenth into the storehouse so that there may be food in my house. Test me in this way," says the Lord of Armies. "See if I will not open the floodgates of heaven and pour out a blessing for you without measure. I will rebuke the devourer for you, so that it will not ruin the produce of your land and your vine in your field will not fail to produce fruit," says the Lord of Armies. "Then all the nations will consider you fortunate, for you will be a delightful land," says the Lord of Armies (Malachi 3:7-12, emphasis added).

Malachi began his case by rehearsing Israel's general disobedience to God:

> "Since the days of your ancestors, you have turned from my statutes; you have not kept them. Return to me, and I will return to you," says the Lord of Armies.

Israel had never been a very obedient people. They were always stubborn and rebellious—a microcosm of all humanity. As Jesus once said, "No one is good, but God alone" (Mark 10:18). And once again, Israel was proving the point, rebelling against God. The Lord called them to return to Him but Israel was skeptical. They weren't ready to admit their guilt. Few people are. It's hard to admit that you have sinned against someone. We all want to believe we are good, God-fearing people who may have flaws, but nothing too serious. The people didn't believe what Malachi said about their rebelliousness. They needed convincing. The prophet put his finger on a specific sin, namely, *theft*:

> "Will a man rob God? Yet you are robbing me!"

The prophet charged Israel with robbing God, but they didn't believe it. It's one thing to take a man's wallet, or donkey, or to break into his house and take his most precious possessions. But how does a man living on earth steal from God in heaven? The Israelites feigned innocence:

"How do we rob you?"

So God got into specifics. Israel had financial obligations they weren't fulfilling. They had to meet the covenantal duties of the Law of Moses.

"By not making the payments of the tenth and the contributions. You are suffering under a curse, yet you—the whole nation—are still robbing me."

God's covenant with Israel promised both curses and blessings. If Israel paid what they owed, God would abundantly bless them. Their lands and vines would be fruitful, and everyone would know that God was prospering them. But there was a penalty for defaulting on their payments. Israel's failure to obey the law triggered the covenantal curses. But there was still time to avoid that. If they repented and stopped robbing God, they could be blessed:

"Bring the full tenth into the storehouse so that there may be food in my house. Test me in this way," says the Lord of Armies. "See if I will not open the floodgates of heaven and pour out a blessing for you without measure. I will rebuke the devourer for you, so that it will not ruin the produce of your land and your vine in your field will not fail to produce fruit," says the Lord of Armies. "Then all the nations will consider you fortunate, for you will be a delightful land," says the Lord of Armies.

If Israel brought all the tithes into the Temple, it would feed the priests, they would enjoy the covenantal blessings, and all nations would know it.

There you have Malachi's warning to Israel.

Many Christian preachers have used Malachi 3 to threaten their congregations. They promised blessings or curses from God based on tithing 10% of their income to the church. "That's what the Bible says," they confidently assert. But is it? Is that really what Malachi 3 says?

Read the passage carefully.

Does Malachi ever tell Israel to give a tenth of their income to anyone?

Not exactly.

Instead, the prophet talks about *the payments of the tenth* and *the contributions*, both of which are in the plural. In other words, there's not *one* payment but *several*!

What are those payments? What were they payments on? How much did Israel owe to God?

Asking those basic questions will help deconstruct the myth of tithing.

Let's look at the evidence together.

ONE

The Myth Examined

1.1. Is Tithing a Myth?

All through my Christian life, preachers have told me to give a tenth of my income to the church. As a young believer, I heard that same message from so many different pastors and teachers that I assumed it must be true and never thought to question it. But when I finally decided to study this issue for myself, I opened my Bible, looked up the passages about tithing, and came to a surprising realization, which I'll share in a moment.

Most of those passages about tithing appear in Leviticus and Deuteronomy. Ordinary Christians rarely read those books, and pastors seldom preach from them. But if you read what they say, I am confident you will conclude that the idea that we should give 10% of our income to the church is a myth.

As we read these passages, remember that Israel was a country. It takes money to run a country. Israel funded itself, like every other nation, through taxes. Just as we have a tax code enforced by the IRS, Biblical Israel had a tax code enforced by the Law of Moses.

However, you may be surprised to learn that Israel's tax code never required giving 10% of your income to the religious authorities. The actual system of giving *was far more complicated*. For example, did you know there were *three tithes* in the Mosaic Law? Yes, three. That's why Malachi referred to "the payments of the tenth." You can read about them in Leviticus 27:30–33, Deuteronomy 14:22–27, and Deuteronomy 14:28–29.

Let's read them together.

1.2. The Levitical Tithe

First, there was the Levitical Tithe. For context, remember that God divided Israel into twelve tribes. He gave land to eleven of the tribes, but not to the tribe of Levi. How did God expect them to survive? By relying on giving from the other eleven tribes:

> "**Every tenth of the land's produce, grain from the soil or fruit from the trees, belongs to the Lord; it is holy to the Lord. If a man decides to redeem any part of this tenth, he must add a fifth to its value. Every tenth animal from the herd or flock, which passes under the shepherd's rod, will be holy to the Lord. He is not to inspect whether it is good or bad, and he is not to make a substitution for it. But if he does make a substitution, both the animal and its substitute will be holy; they cannot be redeemed**" (Leviticus 27:30–33).

The Levitical tithe required giving one-tenth of all one's *agricultural products*. This included vegetables, herbs, grain, and fruit. However, this was only paid from food grown on "the land," i.e., within the border of Israel. That is a crucial qualification that affects how much property was taxed.

Notice, the law was realistic. It recognized that some people lived farther away from the Temple than others, making it harder and costlier for them to transport their crops. Those farmers had the option of substituting crops for cash, but they would have to pay a 20% penalty. Presumably, a Jewish farmer would calculate whether transporting his crops would cost more than the penalty for not doing so and choose the cheaper option.

Meanwhile, if an Israelite raised animals, he had to give one out of every ten animals that "passed under the shepherd's rod." In other words, he had to choose the animal at random. This presumably prevented farmers from tithing their weakest or most undesirable animals.

Notice the interesting math involved with tithing animals. If an Israelite had only nine animals, he wouldn't tithe at all. If he had nineteen, he would tithe one. If he had twenty, he would tithe two.

And here is a surprising fact that helps clarify why the popular teaching about tithing is a myth. According to the law, how much of this tithe would an Israelite pay if he was not a farmer and did not grow crops or raise animals? The answer is none. This was a tax on agricultural products, not income.

1.3. The Festival Tithe

Second, there was the Festival Tithe. This one also helped the Levites, but it had a different purpose from the Levitical Tithe. You can read about it in Deuteronomy:

> "Each year you are to set aside a tenth of all the produce grown in your fields. You are to eat a tenth of your grain, new wine, and fresh oil, and the firstborn of your herd and flock, in the presence of the Lord your God at the place where he chooses to have his name dwell, so that you will always learn to fear the Lord your God. But if the distance is too great for you to carry it, since the place where the Lord your God chooses to put his name is too far away from you and since the Lord your God has blessed you, then exchange it for silver, take the silver in your hand, and go to the place the Lord your God chooses. You may spend the silver on anything you want: cattle, sheep, goats, wine, beer, or anything you desire. You are to feast there in the presence of the Lord your God and rejoice with your family. Do not neglect the Levite within your city gates, since he has no portion or inheritance among you (Deuteronomy 14:22–27).

This tithe was also concerned with agricultural products. But several details show this is a different tithe.

First, instead of tithing from one's herds, an Israelite would give the "*firstborn* of your herd and flock."

Second, this tithe allowed distant Israelites to exchange it for cash, but without paying a penalty. They could take the cash equivalent, travel to Jerusalem, buy the food they would have tithed, and eat it in a communal meal.

Third, while the first tithe was to feed the Levites, the Festival Tithe was eaten by the Israelites in a celebratory potluck. They were encouraged to share with the Levites, but it was not for the priests. It was a feast and a festival to thank the Lord.

Given these differences, most scholars agree that this was a second tithe. However, there is uncertainty about how to calculate what to give in addition to the first tithe. For example, were Israelites compelled to tithe twice, giving 20% of their crops? Or was the second tithe on the 90% left over after paying the first tithe? We're not sure.

But whatever the final percentage, it was almost certainly more than 10%.

1.4. The Poor Tithe

Third, there was the Poor Tithe. Every country has poor citizens. God expected Israel to do something to help them. The Mosaic Law, besides encouraging private charity, provided public aid for the poor.

> "At the end of every three years, bring a tenth of all your produce for that year and store it within your city gates. Then the Levite, who has no portion or inheritance among you, the resident alien, the fatherless, and the widow within your city gates may come, eat, and be satisfied. And the Lord your God will bless you in all the work of your hands that you do (Deuteronomy 14:28–29).

The Poor Tithe was given every three years. Since Israel functioned on a seven-year schedule, this tithe was brought in the third and sixth years and the land would lie fallow in the seventh. Some scholars think the Poor Tithe replaced the first two tithes in those years, but most identify it as a third payment.

Once again, this tithe concerns agricultural products. However, no animals are mentioned. Another difference is that while the first two tithes were brought to the Temple in Jerusalem, this one was paid locally, in the nearest city. Levites lived all over Israel, not just in Jerusalem. So, the Poor Tithe was one way for the other tribes to support local Levites and their families. It also helped local widows, orphans, and resident aliens. (I think everyone in ministry can appreciate how the priests are lumped in with the poor!).

1.5. Adding Up the Tithes

Having reviewed the primary evidence, you should now have a much better idea of what Malachi meant when he blamed Israel for not paying *the payments of the tithe* (plural).

The Mosaic Law required *three tithes*.

Scholars disagree about how to harmonize these payments. When you add them together, an Israelite farmer would pay something like 23.33% of his agricultural products and more if he took the 20% penalty for paying in cash. Notice that I said "agricultural products," not "income." Unlike popular teaching about tithing, none of the three tithes required paying taxes on your income.

1.6. The Other Contributes Required by Law

Americans pay numerous taxes. We pay Federal income tax, State income tax, local property taxes, and sales tax. On top of those, we also pay social security taxes, driver's license fees, vehicle registration fees, and gasoline taxes. I read somewhere that Americans pay about one hundred different taxes and fees to the State.

Israel was similar. So far, we have covered the Mosaic Law's three tithes. But Malachi also faulted Israel for not paying *the contributions*. What were these other payments?

Like most tax systems, it gets complicated.

The following is not a complete list of all the other fees paid by the Israelites.

First, there was the offering of the first fruits. This is where the first portion of the harvest was offered to God (cf. Leviticus 23:10-14). The law required that when the Israelites entered the land, they had to bring the first sheaf of grain from their harvest to the priest. He then waved it on their behalf. This showed that they depended on God for the harvest to come and served as a thank-offering in anticipation of that future harvest.

Second, there was the offering of the firstborn. In Exodus 13:2, 13, families dedicated their firstborn male children and livestock to God. The family could redeem their firstborn son by paying five shekels (Numbers 18:15-16). Firstborn donkeys were swapped for a lamb or a kid because donkeys were unsuitable for sacrifice.

Third, there were freewill offerings. This is where Israelites gave voluntary gifts to the temple or sanctuary (Exodus 35:20-29). They gave anything they wanted. This included garments, jewelry, yarn, precious stones, olive oil, and cash. (As we will see in later chapters, New Testament giving is most like giving freewill offerings.)

Fourth, there were votive offerings. These were items or sacrifices promised to God in fulfillment of a vow (Leviticus 7:16). For example, someone might vow, "Lord, if you help me sail to Rome safely, I will sacrifice a lamb." The worshiper was to present a peace offering when the vow was fulfilled. This was to celebrate with family and friends.

Fifth, Israelites paid a census tax. All men of military age paid a half-shekel each year. This was a ransom for their lives and for the Temple's upkeep (Exodus 30:13-16).

Sixth, the Torah and prophetic writings emphasized regular giving to support the needy (Deuteronomy 15:7-11).

Seventh, every seventh year was considered a Sabbath Year. The land was allowed to rest, and debts were to be forgiven (Leviticus 25:1-7; Deuteronomy 15:1-2). Farmers and debtors would lose income for that year.

Eighth, every 50th year was the Year of Jubilee. In it, the land was to be returned to the original tribe and all slaves were to be freed (Leviticus 25:8-55). It was meant to be a new beginning—a chance to start over. However, you can imagine how costly it would be to give up your farms and homes to another tribe. That is why Israel never kept the Jubilee law. They foresaw the loss. They did not believe God would bless them for their obedience. As punishment, God sent them into exile.

Those were the contributions that Israel had to make under the law. When you add them to the three tithes, the average Israelite's annual tax burden is even higher. However, it should be clear that no laws required Israelites to give 10% of their income to religious authorities.

1.7. Exceptions and Loopholes

Every tax system has its exceptions and loopholes and ancient Israel was no different. How much an Israelite paid depended on who he was, what he did, where he lived, and where he owned assets.

For example, imagine if a Jewish family ran a successful construction business. Let's use American dollars for the illustration. Imagine they made $10,000,000 doing construction. However, they also had a few acres of land that produced about $1,000 worth of barley. What part of their income would be taxable? Under the Mosaic Law, they wouldn't pay any tithes on their millions from construction because it is not an agricultural product. Instead, they would only pay the three tithes out of their $1,000 worth of barley. (They would also pay the other contributions from their total income.)

Now, let's imagine another scenario with three families. The Jacobsons have 7,000 sheep in Syria but only 19 on land in Israel. The Bernsteins have 22 sheep in Israel. And finally, the Goldmans are jewelers with no sheep or land. How much should each family pay?

The Jacobsons wouldn't pay any tithe on the sheep in Syria. They would only tithe on animals in Israel, meaning they would only tithe one sheep.

The Bernsteins have 22 sheep in Israel, so they would tithe two animals.

And since the Goldmans are not farmers, with no agricultural products to speak of, they would not tithe at all.

I hope you see that, contrary to much popular teaching, the Israelites never paid a tithe on their income. That concept does not appear in the Mosaic Law, and no example exists of anyone doing that. Instead, the Israelites paid a complicated series of taxes and payments that primarily applied to farmers. The total percentage due was closer to 23.33%, not 10%.

1.8. Did Abraham Tithe?

Some preachers, undeterred by what the Mosaic Law actually requires, cite Abraham as an early example of tithing your income. But once again, if you read what Abraham did, you will see it is not the same as modern teaching about tithing.

Here is the context.

Abraham journeyed to the Promised Land with his nephew Lot. But as their flocks grew, the land felt increasingly crowded and they decided to part ways (Genesis 13). Lot chose to head towards Sodom—a bad choice! War broke out in the area and during one of the battles, four kings kidnapped Lot and took all his possessions. When Abraham heard about it, he gathered up his fighting men, fought against the kings, and rescued Lot:

> He brought back all the goods and also his relative Lot and his goods, as well as the women and the other people (Genesis 14:16).

Abraham rescued Lot and his goods, but he also brought back the goods he took from the defeated kings. Some time later, a mysterious figure named Melchizedek came out to meet Abraham. He was the king of Salem, a priest to God Most High, and came to bless Abraham. In response, Abraham made an offering:

> And Abram gave him a tenth of everything (Genesis 14:20).

Abraham gave Melchizedek a tenth of everything. Before you assume that he gave Melchizedek 10% of his post-tax income, what is the "everything" here? Hebrews 7 tells us:

> Now consider how great this man was: even Abraham the patriarch gave *a tenth of the plunder to him* (Hebrews 7:4, emphasis added).

Abraham didn't tithe his income but his war loot. He wasn't paying a recurring legal obligation. He was making a one-time free-will offering based on a one-time event. The Bible doesn't record Abraham ever tithing to Melchizedek again, let alone every month or every year. In other words, this isn't an example of tithing as preached today.

The claim that Abraham tithed is another myth.

1.9. Did Jacob Tithe?

In Genesis 28:10-22, Jacob dreamed of an angelic stairway to heaven. The Lord appeared in the dream and promised to watch over him, to give him the land and descendants to live in it. Jacob named the place Bethel and erected a pillar. He vowed that if God kept His promises, he would give to God "a tenth of all that you give me" (Genesis 28:22). This is as close to a tithe as you get in the Old Testament. However, Jacob commits to tithing everything he receives, not just income. And like Abraham's offering to Melchizedek, this is voluntary, not obligatory. It is not a law but a freely chosen expression of gratitude.

1.10. Malachi Revisited

Now that we have examined the Biblical evidence, you can see that no Israelite was required to give 10% of their income to the religious authorities. The more complicated reality is that Israel was to pay three separate tithes. Each had specific rules about what income could be taxed. There were also various mandatory payments, contributions, and offerings. The popular teaching about tithing your income is a myth. It isn't taught in the Mosaic Law.

After researching this evidence, I wondered, "Have the preachers who teach tithing ever studied what the Bible says about it?" The texts are plain to read, and all the mainstream commentaries explain the rules. Why do preachers insist the Bible commands us to give 10% of our income?

I think this is one of those cases where tradition has trumped Scripture. Tithing is a myth.

But, for argument's sake, suppose the Mosaic Law did require that Israelites pay 10% of their income to the religious authorities. Would that law apply to Christians today? Are Christians under the law?

The short answer is no. Christ is the end of the law. In the next chapter, I will explain what that means.

TWO

Christians Are Not Under Law

2.1. Introduction

"I am going to give each one of you pastors the opportunity to repent tonight," the speaker said gravely. The room was quiet. Hundreds of African pastors sat listening with fear and worry on their faces. "Immediately after this convention, go back to your congregations. Make it clear to them: *anyone who is not paying his tithes is not going to heaven. Full stop.*"

No one at the conference objected to that claim.

Not a single pastor.

"Each time you fail to pay your tithes, you're bringing a curse on yourself," he continued. "That's what Adam and Eve did, and God chased them out of the Garden. That's when Immanuel, *God-with-us*, became *God-against-us*. If you fail to pay your tithes, you're calling on God to come and fight you."

Does our salvation depend on paying tithes?

That kind of claim shows a deep flaw in popular tithing teachings: *it mixes law and grace.*

In this chapter, I want to show you that law and grace are different ways of relating to God. I will make clear that Jesus came to free us from the law, including the laws about tithing. We are under grace, not law. Once you're clear about that, you can learn about grace-giving.

2.2. The Contrast Between Law and Grace

Once upon a time, there was no law. There was a time before the Mosaic Law existed. Adam and Eve didn't live under it. Neither did Noah, Abraham, or Joseph. God only gave the law after He sent Moses to rescue the Hebrews from Egyptian slavery. In other words, the law had a historical *beginning*, and it was always meant to have an *ending*. In fact, Jesus ended it and brought something new. As John's Gospel puts it:

> **Indeed, we have all received grace upon grace from his fullness, for the law was given through Moses; grace and truth came through Jesus Christ (John 1:16-17).**

The law was given through Moses, but Jesus brought *grace and truth*.

Think about law and grace as two different religious systems.

A religion focused on law depends on your work, performance, and behavior. In such a system, you will strive to live up to the different demands of the law in your thoughts, words, and deeds. You will constantly judge yourself and others according to that standard, often excusing your own failures, while criticizing others for theirs. This legalistic approach to discipleship eventually leads to self-righteous delusion and legalistic burnout. Unfortunately, many churches and denominations are intensely legalistic. They see discipleship in terms of obeying rules and laws. Telling people to tithe is one example of that approach.

By contrast, Christians live under grace (cf. Romans 6:14). We live life according to a different paradigm. Or, we should.

Since Christians often struggle with legalism and the role of law, let's delve into why Jesus came to save us from the law.

2.3. Everyone Is a Sinner

The law *could* have been a blessing *if anyone had obeyed*. But no one except Jesus ever has. Everyone but Jesus breaks the law. The Israelites should have known that. Day after day, year after year, thousands of animals were sacrificed for the sins of the people, reminding them of their habitual disobedience. The law was a sobering reminder that if God were to judge Israel based on what she had done, no one would be justified, and everyone would be condemned because no one is good.

Sadly, not every Israelite understood the lesson. Some remained stubbornly self-righteous. But other Israelites were humbled by their sinfulness. As David lamented:

> The fool says in his heart, "There's no God."
> They are corrupt; they do vile deeds.
> There is no one who does good.
> The Lord looks down from heaven on the human race
> to see if there is one who is wise,
> one who seeks God.
> All have turned away;
> all alike have become corrupt.
> There is no one who does good,
> not even one (Psalm 14:1-3; cf. Psalm 53:1-3; Romans 3:10-12).

According to David, no one is righteous. Not even one. Everyone breaks the law. So, according to the law, what do covenant breakers deserve?

2.4. The Law Produces Wrath

The law promised *blessings* for those who obeyed, and *curses* for those who disobeyed. As Moses reminded the people.

> "'Anyone who does not put the words of this law into practice is cursed.' And all the people will say, 'Amen!'" (Deuteronomy 27:26).

> "But if you do not obey the LORD your God by carefully following all his commands and statutes I am giving you today, all these curses will come and overtake you" (Deuteronomy 28:15).

The problem is that everyone broke the law—not just once or twice but thousands of times. Thus, all Israelites were under the curse of the law. What did that entail? As Paul put it, it meant getting wrath:

> because the law produces wrath. And where there is no law, there is no transgression (Romans 4:15).

That's what every sinner deserves: wrath.

However, most people have a dull sense of their sinfulness. They don't realize the kind of trouble they are in because of their disobedience. That is why preaching God's wrath was part of the revelation of the gospel. As Paul opened his letter to the Romans, the gospel reveals two things: God's *righteousness* and His *wrath*:

> For I am not ashamed of the gospel, because it is the power of God for salvation to everyone who believes, first to the Jew, and also to the Greek. For in it *the righteousness of God is revealed* from faith to faith, just as it is written: The righteous will live by faith. *For God's wrath is revealed* from heaven against all godlessness and unrighteousness of people who by their unrighteousness suppress the truth (Romans 1:16-18, emphasis).

The gospel reveals that God's wrath and judgment upon sin is coming. The court date has been set and Jesus was appointed as the judge:

> "Therefore, having overlooked the times of ignorance, God now commands all people everywhere to repent, because he has set a day when he is going to judge the world in righteousness by the man he has appointed. He has provided proof of this to everyone by raising him from the dead" (Acts 17:30-31).

This fact has to be revealed, because it is not obvious from simply looking at the world. When you look around, it may seem like God has been letting people get away with sin. The wicked can thrive while the righteous are afflicted all day long (cf. Psalm 73:3-5, 12-14). But we know by revelation that God has not been letting sin go. Instead, He is delaying His judgment until a future day when people *will* finally face the consequences of their wickedness. On that day, all the times it looked like someone was getting away with sin will turn out to have been storing up wrath:

> Because of your hardened and unrepentant heart *you are storing up wrath for yourself in the day of wrath*, when God's righteous judgment is revealed. He will repay each one according to his works: eternal life to those who by persistence in doing good seek glory, honor, and immortality; but wrath and anger to those who are self-seeking and disobey the truth while obeying unrighteousness (Romans 2:5-8, emphasis added).

Everything you have ever done is pictured as being recorded in books, those books will be opened, and every one of your works will be examined (Revelation 20:12). Nothing will be missed. Nothing. Not even a single "idle word" (Matthew 12:36).

If, by chance, someone has earned eternal life through good works, then they will be repaid with eternal life. However, they must have not merely *heard* but actually *obeyed* the law (cf. Romans 2:13). While that is *hypothetically* possible, the reality is that we have broken the law thousands of times, whether in our minds, tongues, or actions. Therefore, the gospel reveals that no one will be justified by works because everyone has fallen short of God's glory (cf. Romans 3:20-23). So what hope of salvation do sinners have?

This is where the good news of the gospel comes in.

God sent Jesus to die for your sins and to pay your penalty. That way, instead of having to be condemned for your works, you can be forgiven and justified through believing in Jesus:

> "Therefore, let it be known to you, brothers and sisters, that through this man forgiveness of sins is being proclaimed to you. Everyone who believes is justified through him from everything that you could not be justified from through the law of Moses" (Acts 13:38-39).

The cross demonstrated God's righteousness. The Lord could not be described as righteous if He simply disregarded all the wickedness in the world. Sin had to be dealt with, and God did that through the cross.[1] God revealed the sinfulness of sin by punishing Jesus for it as our substitute. And having done that, He can then justly show mercy to anyone who believes:

> God presented him as the mercy seat by his blood, through faith, to demonstrate his righteousness, because in his restraint God passed over the sins previously committed. God presented him to demonstrate his righteousness at the present time, so that he would be just and justify the one who has faith in Jesus. Where, then, is boasting? It is excluded. By what kind of law? By one of works? No, on the contrary, by a law of faith. For we conclude that a person is justified by faith apart from the works of the law (Romans 3:25-28).

How does the gospel leave no room for boasting?

Because it makes it clear that everyone deserves condemnation. Everyone failed the test, including you. You deserve wrath and God should condemn you. In fact, as Jesus said, if you do not believe, you are condemned already (John 3:18). If you do not believe, you already have your Last Judgment verdict. But God, in His mercy, saves you from wrath through faith apart from works:

> **The one who believes in the Son has eternal life, but the one who rejects the Son will not see life; instead, the wrath of God remains on him (John 3:36).**

In other words, although the Last Judgment is still future, everyone gets their verdict ahead of time. The options are either eternal life or wrath. If you believe in the Son, you have eternal life. If you reject Him, you have wrath. It's that simple. Do you believe in Jesus?

The good news is since God has already declared believers to be just—since you already have your verdict—you can be sure of being saved from that future day of wrath. As Paul said:

> **But God proves his own love for us in that while we were still sinners, Christ died for us.** *How much more then, since we have now been justified by his blood, will we be saved through him from wrath.* **For if, while we were enemies, we were reconciled to God through the death of his Son, then** *how much more, having been reconciled, will we be saved by his life.* **And not only that, but we also boast in God through our Lord Jesus Christ, through whom we have now received this reconciliation (Romans 5:8-11, emphasis added; cf. Romans 2:5).**

As C. E. B. Cranfield explains, "The point made is that, since God has already done the really difficult thing, that is, justified impious sinners, we may be absolutely confident that He will do what is by comparison very easy, namely, save from His wrath at the last those who are already righteous in His sight."[2]

Another reason believers can be confident that we *are* saved now and *will be* saved later is that Jesus said the Father gave Him the authority to judge, and He already promised not to judge believers:

> **"The Father, in fact, judges no one but** *has given all judgment to the Son*, **so that all people may honor the Son just as they honor the Father. Anyone who does not honor the Son does not honor the Father who sent him. Truly I tell you, anyone who hears my word and believes him who sent me has eternal life** *and will not come under judgment* **but has passed from death to life" (John 5:22-24, emphasis added).**

Are you afraid of God's judgment? Are you unsure of how to be saved? Know that Jesus is the judge with the authority to give the verdict. And He has decided that salvation depends on believing in Him. If you believe, then there will be no judgment for you.

Salvation is by grace through faith, apart from works (cf. Ephesians 2:8-9).

But not everyone agrees.

Some people—even people who claim to be Christian—*hate* this message. They do! They call it heresy, Satanic, easy believism, and oppose it whenever they can.

What is the alternative?

If someone rejects salvation by faith *apart from works*, they must believe in a salvation that *depends on works*. There's no other option. And if someone believes *that*, they must think they're either already good enough to be saved or they can be if only they try a little harder. In other words, the person who believes in works salvation is spiritually deluded and needs to be convinced about how deep their sinfulness goes before they will be open to hearing the faith-alone gospel. They don't realize the truth of the evidence we have already looked at. But how do you convince anyone of their sinfulness? How do you bring them to that point of despairing in their own righteousness?

That's where the law comes in.

2.5. The Law Teaches Our Need for a Savior

I started lifting weights about two years ago, at the age of forty-four. I always considered myself stronger than average, even without working out, but when I began testing myself against a powerlifting program, I quickly realized how weak I was!

That's what tests can do. They can correct false impressions and help us face the reality of the situation.

That's also what the law can do.

No one will be *saved* through the law. That is not its purpose. But it still has an important lesson to teach:

> **For no one will be justified in his sight by the works of the law, because *the knowledge of sin comes through the law* (Romans 3:20, emphasis added).**

The law reveals your sin. It shines a big, bright spotlight on it. How does it do that? By giving you a test that you flunk.

I used to think I was strong until I tried deadlifting 400 lbs. Now I know better!

Likewise, when the law tells you to do something ("Thou shall not covet!"), and you keep failing to obey it no matter how hard you try, you'll finally realize just how deep the sin goes. It isn't an accident or mistake but something living with you in your body (Romans 7:23).

Not convinced? Then consider the command to love.

Jesus said that love summarizes the whole law—the whole duty of man to God and his neighbors. You should love God with all your heart, mind, soul, and strength and love your neighbor as yourself. If you expect to be saved based on your works, then you better be loving, right? But are you? Before you say "yes," consider what it means to love someone:

> **Love is patient, love is kind. Love does not envy, is not boastful, is not arrogant, is not rude, is not self-seeking, is not irritable, and does not keep a record of wrongs. Love finds no joy in unrighteousness but rejoices in the truth. It bears all things, believes all things, hopes all things, endures all things (1 Corinthians 13:4-7).**

You might think you're loving, but measure yourself against Paul's standard. Have you ever been impatient or mean? Have you ever been envious, boastful, arrogant, rude, or self-seeking? Have you ever been irritable with your kids or spouse? Have you ever reminded your husband, wife, or children about that bad thing they did months or years ago? Have you ever enjoyed sinning just a little or been less than truthful? Have you ever complained about your recent struggles? Or have you doubted, despaired, or wanted to give up?

If so, then you haven't loved.

After reading Paul's description of what it means to love, do you still think that you're a loving person? Personally, I always wonder, "Have I ever loved anyone in my entire life?"

That is what the law does. It shines a spotlight on your sins to make you understand your true situation before God and to help you realize that if you're going to be saved, it will have to be by some other way apart from the law.

Enter the gospel.

Paul compares the law to a legal guardian there to teach us that we need Jesus and justification by faith:

> **The law, then, was our guardian until Christ, so that we could be justified by faith (Galatians 3:24).**

In other words, the law had a temporary role and an endpoint. It was to last until Jesus came so that we could be justified before God, not based on our works, but by faith. The law was meant to lead people to the gospel.

2.6. Jesus Became a Curse for Us

How did the Lord save us from the law? It goes back to the question of the law's curses. Since man could not save himself, the Son of God became a man. The Word became flesh, was born under the law, and obeyed it for us (cf. John 1:14; Galatians 4:4). He fulfilled His covenantal obligations (Matthew 5:17) and therefore earned the blessings of the law. In fact, older Christian writers understood Psalm 1 to be a prophecy about Jesus, i.e., He is the man who fulfills the law and is blessed.

Jesus not only fulfilled the law by obeying it, but also paid our penalty for breaking it.

For centuries, the Israelites were commanded to make substitutionary animal sacrifices. They learned that sin was punishable by death. But according to the logic of sacrifice, a life could be substituted for a life. That is what Jesus did for us: He became the Lamb of God who takes away the world's sins (John 1:29) and substituted His life for ours. When He went to the cross, our sins were transferred to Him:

He himself bore our sins in his body on the tree; so that, having died to sins, we might live for righteousness. By his wounds you have been healed (1 Peter 2:24; cf. Isaiah 53:5-6).

When our sins were imputed to Christ on the cross, He took the curse of the law upon Himself. In Paul's words, He became a curse for us:

Christ redeemed us from the curse of the law by becoming a curse for us, because it is written, Cursed is everyone who is hung on a tree (Galatians 3:13).

And when Jesus took our curse upon Himself, He redeemed us from the law's curse.

Jesus' death had different benefits for different people. For example, He is the propitiation for the sins of the world (1 John 2:2). But even though Jesus died for the world's sins, that doesn't mean the world is automatically saved. The Lord made a complete *provision* for our salvation through His death and resurrection but the application of the provision requires a response from us.

2.7. Saved by Faith Apart from Works

To be saved, there is only one thing that people can do: *believe in Jesus*. Faith, not works, is how God applies the provision of the cross to you. That is the basis of salvation by grace. And if you understand and believe this, it helps you recognize so much false teaching about tithing.

I could cite dozens of verses supporting the doctrine of salvation by faith, but here is a sampling. Please read these slowly and pay attention to the italicized parts. They either emphasize *believing* or exclude *working* as the condition of salvation:

> "But to all who did receive him, he gave them the right to be children of God, *to those who believe in his name*" (John 1:12, emphasis added).

> "Just as Moses lifted up the snake in the wilderness, so the Son of Man must be lifted up, so that *everyone who believes in him* may have eternal life" (John 3:14-15, emphasis added).

> For we conclude that a person is justified *by faith apart from the works of the law* (Romans 3:28, emphasis added).

> But to the one who *does not work*, but *believes on him* who declares the ungodly to be righteous, his faith is credited for righteousness (Romans 4:5, emphasis added).

> This is why the promise is *by faith*, so that it may be according to *grace*, to guarantee it to all the descendants—not only to those who are of the law but also to those who are of Abraham's faith. He is the father of us all (Romans 4:16, emphasis added).

> Therefore, since we have been *justified by faith*, we have peace with God through our Lord Jesus Christ (Romans 5:1, emphasis added).

> What should we say then? Gentiles, who did not pursue righteousness, have attained righteousness, namely *the righteousness that comes from faith*. But Israel, pursuing the law of righteousness, has not achieved the righteousness of the law.

Why is that? *Because they did not pursue it by faith*, but as if it were *by works*. They stumbled over the stumbling stone (Romans 9:30, emphasis added).

Yet we know that *no one is justified by the works of the law* but *by faith in Jesus Christ*. And we have *believed* in Christ Jesus so that we might be *justified by faith* in Christ and *not by the works of the law*, because *by the works of the law no human being will be justified* (Galatians 2:16, emphasis added).

For you are saved *by grace through faith*, and this is not from yourselves; it is God's gift—*not from works*, so that no one can boast (Ephesians 2:8-9, emphasis added)

Do you see that believing in Jesus is the only condition of salvation? This is not an obscure doctrine found in one or two verses but written clearly and repeatedly across the New Testament.

Salvation is by grace, not law. But so is the whole of the Christian life.

2.8. Christians Are Released from the Law

As I said, Jesus' death had multiple benefits, one of which is that He freed us from the law. We have seen the Biblical function of the law, and how it reveals our sinfulness and need for a Savior. We have also seen that salvation is by faith, not law. Now it is important to see we are no longer under law at all. How did that happen?

As you know, it is a general legal principle that a contract is only valid so long as the person is alive. For example, consider marriage. You and your spouse are obligated to each other so long as you both shall live but when either spouse dies, the other can remarry.

Paul uses that legal principle to explain why Christians are no longer under law. As he explains:

Since I am speaking to those who know the law, brothers and sisters, don't you know that the law rules over someone as long as he lives? For example, a married woman is legally bound to her husband while he lives. But if her husband dies, she is released from the law regarding the husband. So then, if she is married to another man while her husband is living, she will be called an adulteress. But if her husband dies, she is free from that law. Then, if she is married to another man, she is not an adulteress (Romans 7:1-3).

There is the standard legal principle that death ends the marriage obligation. How does that apply to Christians and the law? Aren't we still alive?

Therefore, my brothers and sisters, you also were put to death in relation to the law through the body of Christ so that you may belong to another. You belong to him who was raised from the dead in order that we may bear fruit for God (Romans 7:4).

In Paul's illustration, Christians were married to the law. But then a death occurred that freed us to marry someone else. The odd part of the illustration is that you would expect the law to die so the Christian can remarry. But the Christian died instead. How did that happen? It happened when we were united to Christ as members of His body. We became one in His death and resurrection (cf. Romans 6:3-11). That death means Christians are released from the law:

But now we have been released from the law, since we have died to what held us, so that we may serve in the newness of the Spirit and not in the old letter of the law (Romans 7:6).

Being freed from the law means we can serve in a new way, "in the newness of the Spirit," and not "the old letter of the law." *That includes the old letter about tithing (and other payments).* Insofar as Christians are required to give, it is in the newness of the Spirit. The law is not our standard or guide. Something much better has come.

2.9. Christians Enjoy the New Covenant

Pastors who tell their congregations they are obliged to tithe make the fundamental mistake of thinking we're still under law instead of grace. Christ has freed us from the law. It is no longer our standard of living, including our standard of giving.

Another way to understand our relationship to the Mosaic Law is this: we are under the New Covenant. God promised one was coming:

"Look, the days are coming"—this is the Lord's declaration—"when I will make a new covenant with the house of Israel and with the house of Judah. This one will not be like the covenant I made with their ancestors on the day I took them by the hand to lead them out of the land of Egypt—my

covenant that they broke even though I am their master"—the Lord's declaration. "Instead, this is the covenant I will make with the house of Israel after those days"—the Lord's declaration. "I will put my teaching within them and write it on their hearts. I will be their God, and they will be my people. No longer will one teach his neighbor or his brother, saying, 'Know the Lord,' for they will all know me, from the least to the greatest of them"—this is the Lord's declaration. "For I will forgive their iniquity and never again remember their sin. (Jeremiah 31:31-34).

This covenant would be different, not just in terms, but in kind. In part, the covenant participants themselves would be different. Hearts would be changed. God would do a work within them.

This was also prophesied by Ezekiel:

I will also sprinkle clean water on you, and you will be clean. I will cleanse you from all your impurities and all your idols. I will give you a new heart and put a new spirit within you; I will remove your heart of stone and give you a heart of flesh. I will place my Spirit within you and cause you to follow my statutes and carefully observe my ordinances (Ezekiel 36:25-27; Psalm 51:7, 12).

Pay close attention to Ezekiel's language because we will see it again in a conversation between Jesus and Nicodemus. According to Ezekiel, people would be sprinkled with water. They would be cleansed from all impurities. Their stony hearts would be replaced with hearts of flesh and the Spirit would dwell in them.

With that prophecy in mind, here is what Jesus told Nicodemus:

Jesus answered, "Truly I tell you, unless someone is born of water and the Spirit, he cannot enter the kingdom of God. Whatever is born of the flesh is flesh, and whatever is born of the Spirit is spirit. Do not be amazed that I told you that you must be born again. The wind blows where it pleases, and you hear its sound, but you don't know where it comes from or where it is going. So it is with everyone born of the Spirit" (John 3:5-8).

Recognize the imagery? Nicodemus didn't understand what Jesus was saying, but the Lord expected him to, probably due to the promise in Ezekiel.[3] Jesus was telling Nicodemus the promised New Covenant had finally arrived. That is what the Lord's Supper signifies and declares:

> In the same way he also took the cup after supper and said, "This cup is the new covenant in my blood, which is poured out for you" (Luke 22:20).

Each week, Christians eat the bread and drink the wine, remembering the New Covenant that Jesus cut with His blood.

In fact, Paul contrasted this New Covenant ministry with the law's ministry saying that he was a minister of the New Covenant:

> He has made us competent *to be ministers of a new covenant*, not of the letter, but of the Spirit. For the letter kills, but the Spirit gives life. Now if the ministry that brought death, chiseled in letters on stones, came with glory, so that the Israelites were not able to gaze steadily at Moses's face because of its glory, which was set aside, how will the ministry of the Spirit not be more glorious? For if the ministry that brought condemnation had glory, the ministry that brings righteousness overflows with even more glory. In fact, what had been glorious is not glorious now by comparison because of the glory that surpasses it. For if what was set aside was glorious, what endures will be even more glorious (2 Corinthians 3:6-11, emphasis added).

What does this mean for how we understand giving?

The complex laws about tithing belong to the ministry that brought death. Malachi 3 is evidence of the curses that came with the law. But the New Covenant ministry of the Spirit is different. While the Mosaic Law had a certain kind of glory, the New Covenant is much more glorious. As the writer of Hebrews says, it is far superior:

> But Jesus has now obtained a superior ministry, and to that degree he is the mediator of a better covenant, which has been established on better promises. For if that first covenant had been faultless, there would have been no occasion for a second one…By saying a new covenant, he has declared that the first is obsolete. And what is obsolete and growing old is about to pass away (Hebrews 8:6-7, 13).

We are in the New Covenant, which is a better one. The first covenant is obsolete. That means the old laws about tithing are obsolete, too. Mosaic tithing is not the Christian's standard for giving.

2.10. Conclusion

The last chapter showed that tithing is a myth. This chapter has shown that, even if the law did command tithing, Christians are under grace, not law, saved through faith apart from works, and are participants in the New Covenant, not the obsolete Old Covenant.

What does that mean for giving?

When preachers use the Mosaic Law to prove that Christians must tithe, they fail to understand that Christ has redeemed us from the law, including what it commanded about giving.

Yes, Christians should give, but we do so from the perspective of grace, not law. We serve in the newness of the Spirit, not the oldness of the letter. In the next chapter, we will review some of those elements of the newness of grace-giving.

Endnotes

1. James D. G. Dunn, *Romans 1–8* (Dallas, TX: Word, 1988), 267.
2. C. E. B. Cranfield, *A Critical and Exegetical Commentary on the Epistle to the Romans* (Edinburgh: T & T Clark, 1975), 1:266; cf. Anders Nygren, *Commentary on Romans*, trans. Carl C. Rasmussen (Philadelphia, PA: Muhlenberg Press, 1949), 203-204; John Stott, *Romans: God's Good News for the World* (Downers Grove, IL: InterVarsity, 1994), 146.
3. Leonhard Goppelt, *Typos: The Typological Interpretation of the Old Testament in the New*, trans. Donald H. Madvig (Grand Rapids, MI: Eerdmans, 1982), 182.

THREE
Principles of Grace Giving

3.1. Introduction

Did you have a nickname growing up? Nicknames are usually given not chosen. I don't know if Allan Law wanted to become known as The Sandwich Man, but that is what the people of Minneapolis call him, and he's earned it.

Every single night, after the shelters have closed, when no more public resources are available, he drives around the Twin Cities in a van emblazoned with the words "Love One Another," giving out sandwiches, gloves, and blankets to the poorest of the poor.

One year, he gave out 520,000 sandwiches!

A team of volunteers makes them. It takes six people about 30 minutes to prepare 150 sandwiches, for a total cost of approximately $100. Each of those sandwiches helps a hungry person.

Is there any Biblical command that requires giving out 520,000 sandwiches a year?

No. And yet he does it anyway.

What motivates someone to do that?

That's an important question raised by the explosive truth that Christians are under grace, not law, for giving. We have no obligation to tithe, but it is good to give, so what is our motivation? What kind of guidance do we have?

In this chapter, I will survey some of the basic principles of grace-giving. We will see that while the Old Covenant had very specific rules, percentages, and timelines around giving, the New Covenant is open and free. However, there are rules of thumb to help guide your giving, beginning with who to give your money to.

3.2. Give Where You're Fed

Since there is no longer any Levitical priesthood or Jewish Temple to support, where should Christians give their money?

Here is the first principle of grace giving:

Let the one who is taught the word share all his good things with the teacher (Galatians 6:6).

Paul recommends giving to your teacher. Whoever you go to with your questions about what to believe and how to live as a Christian, whoever teaches you regularly from the Bible, is someone you should support. In other words, *give where you're fed*.

For most people, that means giving to your local church, where your pastor, Sunday school teachers, and small groups leaders teach you. But it can also mean supporting the writers, speakers, radio ministries, podcasters, publishers, and missionaries who teach you the Word and help you grow.

It's right to support Bible teachers financially, not because you must, because it's the law, or because the gospel comes at a price, but because you are grateful that they have shared the word with you. Out of gratitude, you then share good things with them.

If a teacher feeds you with the gospel, avoid dining and dashing and give where you're fed.

3.3. Give What You Can

There is significant flexibility about *who* to support with your giving and there is just as much about *how much* to give. The question is naturally asked, even though you're not obliged to give 10% of your income, should you give *at least* that much?

I think that way of framing the question assumes too much of a law mentality. Paul suggests a different approach.

In 2 Corinthians, Paul told the Corinthians about the funds he was collecting for the suffering saints in Jerusalem. He had already collected money from the churches in Macedonia (e.g., in Philippi, Thessalonica, and Berea), which was surprising because the Macedonians were suffering, too! They were being persecuted (cf. Acts 16:20; Philippians 1:29-30; 1 Thessalonians 1:6; 2:14; 3:3-4), probably leading to their poverty. And yet, despite their suffering, they wanted to help their brothers and sisters in Jerusalem:

> We want you to know, brothers and sisters, about the grace of God that was given to the churches of Macedonia: During a severe trial brought about by affliction, their abundant joy and their extreme poverty overflowed in a wealth of generosity on their part. I can testify that, *according to their ability and even beyond their ability, of their own accord*, they begged us earnestly for the privilege of sharing in the ministry to the saints, and not just as we had hoped. Instead, they gave themselves first to the Lord and then to us by God's will. So we urged Titus that just as he had begun, so he should also complete among you this act of grace (2 Corinthians 8:1-6, emphasis added).

How much did Macedonians give? It was a matter of freedom. Paul didn't require a percentage. Instead, he says they gave "according to their ability," "beyond their ability," and "of their own accord." In other words, they gave what they could. Some gave sacrificially. And they did it freely, without being forced to.

Paul held the Macedonians up as an example for the Corinthians to follow, for they illustrate a key principle of grace-based giving. Instead of thinking in terms of tithes or some other fixed percentage, *give what you can.*

How much can you give? That's for your to decide. No one can do it for you. It depends entirely on your circumstances and your conscience before God.

3.4. Give According to Your Prosperity

The role of the individual conscience in deciding how much to give is also evident in what Paul told the Corinthians when he made his first collection for the saints in Jerusalem:

> On the first day of the week, each of you is to set something aside and save in keeping with how he is prospering, so that no collections will need to be made when I come (1 Corinthians 16:2).

Paul instructed the Corinthians to set some money aside on the first day of the week (i.e., Sunday), when they presumably gathered for corporate worship. Paul was being practical. He wanted the donation to be ready when he arrived. In other words, Paul gave the Corinthians specific instructions about a particular project, not a rule to be followed for all time by all churches. It would be wrong to take this one instance and turn it into a law to be obeyed by all. Churches are not obliged to collect money every Sunday. They are free to make a regular Sunday collection if they so choose, but it is a matter of Christian liberty, not necessity.

Moreover, notice that Paul didn't tell the Corinthians how much to give. He didn't say, "Give at least 10% of your income for the Jerusalem church." He left the amount given open in two ways.

First, Paul left it open for each person to decide how much they were prospering. He told them to give according to their prosperity but didn't define it for them, leaving it to individuals to decide for themselves.

Have you ever wondered if you're prospering? It's all about perspective. If you compare yourself to people who are richer than you, you might think of yourself as poor. There is always someone with a higher-paying job, a newer car, a bigger house, going on a more luxurious vacation. Even multi-millionaires can feel poor compared to billionaires like Elon Musk, Warren Buffet, and the Walton family.

However, Paul calls us to give in light of suffering Christians who need it. If someone asks you to consider your prosperity in light of desperately poor believers, your perspective will flip, and you'll realize that you're one of the "haves" who can help the "have-nots." Comparing yourself to suffering believers can help you see how much you have prospered, which can then motivate you to being more generous with the poor.

Second, Paul also left open how much each person should give out of their prosperity. There was no minimum or maximum required. You are free to give a percentage, a lump sum, or nothing at all if you don't think you're prospering. The apostle left it to the individual conscience.

I sometimes hear people insist giving 10% is a good minimum for giving but we should give more, never less. I disagree with that way of approaching the question. It assumes that grace is a more demanding form of law, which is the exact wrong way to think about it. Under grace, you are free to give according to your conscience, proportionate to how you believe God has prospered you. If you're having a tight month and if you're down to your last dollar, don't feel obliged to give. God isn't going to condemn you or love you less based on your giving. Under grace, give what you can, not what you must.

3.5. Give to Help the Poor

Clearly, grace givers should support their local gospel teachers. But what other kinds of giving should we prioritize? Paul's collection for the saints in Jerusalem points to a second important cause: giving to help the poor.

When Paul presented his gospel message to the apostles in Jerusalem, they acknowledged his mission from the Lord, and gave him their blessing, but with one request:

> When James, Cephas, and John—those recognized as pillars— acknowledged the grace that had been given to me, they gave the right hand of fellowship to me and Barnabas, agreeing that we should go to the Gentiles and they to the circumcised. *They asked only that we would remember the poor, which I had made every effort to do* (Galatians 2:9-10, emphasis added).

Have you ever thought that preaching the gospel and helping the poor *go together*? The apostles did. And so did Paul. He was eager to do just that. Do you remember the poor in that way?

Praise God that Christians have long supported the poor through funding orphanages, hospitals, water well projects, and schools, not to mention sending relief to people suffering from famine or as refugees in war-torn areas. Yes, there's always more to be done, and you should continue thinking about giving to those causes. Wherever the gospel is preached, make every effort to remember the poor with your giving, too.

If you need an added incentive to remember the poor, consider this Proverb:

> Kindness to the poor is a loan to the LORD, and he will give a reward to the lender (Proverbs 19:17).

Giving to the poor is like lending to God. He will reward you for it (and, I imagine, pay you back with interest!).

3.6. Give to Promote Equality

Christians are free to give, but whenever you give, you always have a goal in mind. What kind of goals should grace givers hope to achieve? Paul explained one of the reasons like this:

> It is not that there should be relief for others and hardship for you, but it is a question of equality. *At the present time your*

surplus is available for their need, so that their abundance may in turn meet your need, in order that there may be equality. As it is written: The person who had much did not have too much, and the person who had little did not have too little (2 Corinthians 8:13-15, emphasis added).

Have you ever wondered why God would prosper you? It's easy to think it's for your own leisure and enjoyment. Doesn't God want you to spend your extra money on luxury goods for yourself? But Paul calls us to think differently about excess cash and to take a larger view of our resources as belonging first to God and then to the wider family of God.

You may be prospering now but that might not last, just as other Christians are lacking now but may prosper later. In other words, our relative prosperity can and will change over time, and the position of giver and receiver can be reversed. That's all part of God's plan. In Paul's time, the Corinthians' abundance could meet the Jerusalemites' needs, and one day, the reverse might be true. Therefore, it is prudent to give so as to *promote equality* between brethren during hard times.

To be clear, Paul was not establishing a new law for the churches. He was not imposing socialism, communism, or redistribution as the church's official policy. Paul didn't put into place any mechanism that would require this giving ever to happen again let alone regularly. He simply urges them to give voluntarily, from the heart, according to the leading of the Spirit, with the understanding that your present prosperity often has the purpose of meeting another believer's need.

3.7. Take Precautions with Giving

Where does your charitable giving go? Are you sure it is going to the right people, and being spent on the right causes? Michael Eaton, a British theologian who ministered in Africa, once complained, "wealthy Christians are not very skillful at asking questions and finding out where their money goes."[1] We send out our checks and then stop caring about what happens to the money. Should that be a concern for grace-givers?

When Paul took a large sum of money to Jerusalem, he wanted to take every precaution to ensure the gift arrived safely, so he enlisted Titus and another brother to help Paul deliver the money:

Thanks be to God, who put the same concern for you into the heart of Titus. For he welcomed our appeal and, being very

diligent, went out to you by his own choice. We have sent with him the brother who is praised among all the churches for his gospel ministry. And not only that, but he was also appointed by the churches *to accompany us with this gracious gift* that we are administering for the glory of the Lord himself and to show our eagerness to help. *We are taking this precaution so that no one will criticize us about this large sum that we are administering* (2 Corinthians 8:16-20, emphasis added).

If something were to happen to the donation—if it was misspent, lost, or stolen—potential donors might use that as an excuse to never give again. Paul evidently wanted this to be a continuing practice, but that would only happen if donors trusted the process, so he took every precaution to ensure it went smoothly.

Sadly, there's always a news headline about a pastor stealing money or a ministry tricking gullible donors out of millions. Frankly, you should always beware of religious con artists. Avoid giving to ministries that are careless or irresponsible with their finances. Use a service such as Charity Navigator or Guidestar to vet ministries you are considering supporting. When you give, do not be ashamed or embarrassed about taking the necessary precautions so that your giving is put to the best use.

Grace-giving is careful, not careless.

3.8. Think Carefully About Giving

Under the Mosaic Law, Israelites were told *who* to give to, *what* to give, *when* to give it, *how* to give it, and *why* to give it. But once it was given, they weren't responsible for what happened afterward—that was the priests' business. All in all, the Israelites did not have to do too much thinking. They mostly needed to obey.

By contrast, because grace-givers have so much freedom in giving, they have more to think about:

> And not only that, but he was also appointed by the churches to accompany us with this gracious gift that we are administering for the glory of the Lord himself and to show our eagerness to help. We are taking this precaution so that no one will criticize us about this large sum that we are administering. Indeed, *we are giving careful thought* to do what is right, not only before the Lord but also before people (2 Corinthians 8:19-21, emphasis added).

Grace-givers must decide how much to give, when to give it, whom to give it to, and for which purpose. It is all a matter of freedom, which means it requires much more personal responsibility. You want to make sure your giving is accomplishing the purposes you have set for it. That means it takes careful thought and wisdom.

When you give from the heart, you need to use your head.

3.9. Sow Generously to Reap Generously

Giving makes an obvious difference to the people who receive the gift. The hungry are fed, the naked are clothed, and the homeless are given shelter. But giving also makes a difference to the giver. How?

God seems to have created the world with certain cause-and-effect principles that apply to giving, such as several Scriptures point to a law of "sowing and reaping." For example, Solomon once noted:

> **One person gives freely,**
> **yet gains more;**
> **another withholds what is right,**
> **only to become poor (Proverbs 11:24).**

You might have assumed the opposite would be true and that generous givers become poorer while misers become rich. But that's not what Solomon saw and not what Paul expected.

As the apostle collected funds for the believers in Jerusalem, he encouraged the Corinthians to give all the more by appealing to the principle of sowing and reaping:

> **But I am sending the brothers so that our boasting about you in this matter would not prove empty, and so that you would be ready just as I said. Otherwise, if any Macedonians come with me and find you unprepared, we, not to mention you, would be put to shame in that situation. Therefore I considered it necessary to urge the brothers to go on ahead to you and arrange in advance the generous gift you promised, so that it will be ready as a gift and not as an extortion. The point is this:** *The person who sows sparingly will also reap sparingly, and the person who sows generously will also reap generously* **(2 Corinthians 9:3-6, emphasis added).**

Just as Solomon observed that generous givers seem to prosper, Paul says the generous sowers will reap generously.

Take my garden as an illustration. I'm a bad gardener, but if I've learned anything, it's that if I only plant a few pepper seeds, then I'll only get a few pepper. But if I plant many, I'll get many. That's a natural law of gardening. Apparently, it is also a natural law of grace-giving. If you only give a little money to ministry, you'll only reap little, but if you give generously, then you'll reap generously.

However, before you mistake Paul as teaching some extreme form of prosperity theology, look at the reason why God will prosper you:

> **And God is able to make every grace overflow to you, so that in every way, always having everything you need, you may excel in every good work (2 Corinthians 9:8).**

What is the purpose of reaping generously? Is it so that you can become more comfortable, indulgent, lazy, and live the American dream? No! It is so that you can give even more to those in need. God's blessings overflow to you so you can "excel in every good work."

What does a farmer do with his acres of peppers? The purpose is not to keep them all for himself. If he did, they would only rot and go to waste. Instead, he harvests more peppers than he could ever use for himself so that other people can eat them. The abundance of peppers is to benefit others.

Similarly, Paul is saying that you give generously, to reap generously so that you can give even more to support the work of the gospel and help the poor.

3.10. Give to Inspire Others

Grace-giving depends on the motivations of the heart. But how can you get motivated? People are often reluctant to give, which is why so many pastors teach tithing as legal obligation. The problem is that preaching law usually has the opposite effect. As Paul explained in Romans 7, rather than inspiring obedience, sin uses the commandments to provoke disobedience (cf. Romans 7:9). How can grace-giving avoid that trap? That is, how can it motivate giving without making it into a self-defeating law?

Paul noted that one of the powerful motivations for grace giving is seeing the example of other givers:

> **Now concerning the ministry to the saints, it is unnecessary for me to write to you. For I know your eagerness, and I boast about you to the Macedonians, "Achaia has been ready since**

last year," *and your zeal has stirred up most of them* (2 Corinthians 9:1-2, emphasis added).

When you see other believers giving zealously, out of genuine concern for their suffering brethren, without any law demanding they do it, you will be inspired to give, too. And then your generous giving will stir up other to give, all apart from the motivations of the law.

3.11. Give to Inspire Praise

Another reason to give under grace is to inspire others to glorify God. If you meet a starving person on the street, they generally will not be impressed with your knowledge of the gap theory in Genesis 1, the sacramental theology of 16th century Anabaptists, or the scholarly debates over how much prophecy was fulfilled by the destruction of Jerusalem in AD 70. But they will praise God when you put your faith into action:

> **For the ministry of this service is not only supplying the needs of the saints but is also overflowing in many *expressions of thanks to God*. Because of the proof provided by this ministry, *they will glorify God* for your obedient confession of the gospel of Christ, and for your generosity in sharing with them and with everyone. And as they pray on your behalf, *they will have deep affection for you* because of the surpassing grace of God in you. Thanks be to God for his indescribable gift! (2 Corinthians 9:12-15).**

According to this passage, helping the poor has three effects, all of which relate to how the saints in Jerusalem would respond to God in different sorts of prayer.

First, by supplying their needs, the poverty-stricken saints in Jerusalem would *give thanks to God*.

Second, the saints in Jerusalem would *glorify God* for their the "proof provided by this ministry" through their "obedient confession of the gospel." Proof of what? Perhaps Paul thinks the gift would dispel any doubts among the church in Jerusalem that the Gentiles in Corinth believed the gospel and were church members. Or maybe it would prove the Corinthians had not only heard the word but had become doers of it (cf. James 1:22-25).

Third, the gift would inspire the saints in Jerusalem to *pray to God* on behalf of the Corinthians. The longer I walk with Christ, the more I realize how much every good thing is made possible and empowered by prayer.

If you have ever given sacrificially, you probably already know that one of the most gratifying things about giving is seeing the relief, joy, and thankfulness on the face of the person you have helped. Do you see how motivating that can be? And do you also see how different that motivation is from the threats of the law?

3.12. Give As You Want to Be Given To

One of the most difficult principles of giving under the New Covenant is this one:

> "You have heard that it was said, An eye for an eye and a tooth for a tooth. But I tell you, don't resist an evildoer. On the contrary, if anyone slaps you on your right cheek, turn the other to him also. As for the one who wants to sue you and take away your shirt, let him have your coat as well. And if anyone forces you to go one mile, go with him two. *Give to the one who asks you, and don't turn away from the one who wants to borrow from you*" (Matthew 5:38-42, emphasis added).

Under the Mosaic Law, a victim could seek justice within proportional limits ("an eye for an eye"). But Jesus' followers were to be different. We do not retaliate. That applies to being abused, such as being slapped. But Jesus also mentions giving to people who ask you for things, including to borrow things. We should give it to them. In other words, Christians should be lenders. But we do not lend the way the world does. As Jesus also taught:

> "Give to everyone who asks you, and from someone who takes your things, don't ask for them back. Just as you want others to do for you, do the same for them" (Luke 6:30-31).

If someone takes something from you—which sounds like theft—you are not to ask for it back. This is a difficult saying. Jesus seems to recommend indiscriminate giving to whoever asks for something. How practical is His command?

If any bank put Jesus' policy into practice, it would go out of business. If countries tried this, their markets would collapse. Lending without expecting repayment does not make for a sustainable economic policy. Maybe that is why Christians are called to live by faith.

Understood more generally, Jesus was simply applying the golden rule to giving. He asks you to put yourself in the shoes of a borrower and imagine if you went to someone for help. How would you want to be treated? That's how a grace lender should treat a borrower.

3.13. Lend Without Expecting to Be Repaid

Grace-giving includes lending. The Mosaic Law had rules about borrowing and lending. As we saw, the Year of Jubilee was an extreme example of annulling debts (a law that was never obeyed!). Similarly, Jesus taught that we should lend without expecting to make a profit—indeed, without expecting to get anything back at all:

> "If you lend to those from whom you expect to receive, what credit is that to you? Even sinners lend to sinners to be repaid in full. But love your enemies, do what is good, and lend, *expecting nothing in return*. Then your reward will be great, and you will be children of the Most High. For he is gracious to the ungrateful and evil" (Luke 6:34-35, emphasis added).

Since even sinners lend at a profit, Christians should do better and not expect anything back. I imagine that would make it very hard for Christians to be bankers and obey the Lord in this matter.

3.14. Give Secretly

Christians are strongly encouraged to give. But at the same time, Jesus says we should do it without fanfare:

> "Be careful not to practice your righteousness in front of others to be seen by them. Otherwise, you have no reward with your Father in heaven. So whenever you give to the poor, don't sound a trumpet before you, as the hypocrites do in the synagogues and on the streets, to be applauded by people. Truly I tell you, they have their reward. But when you give to the poor, don't let your left hand know what your right hand is doing, so that your giving may be in secret. And your Father who sees in secret will reward you (Matthew 6:1-4).

Motives are important under grace-giving. We should never be motivated by self-righteousness or the applause of others. So, instead of giving in public, we should give secretly. As Jesus put it, "don't let your left hand know what your right hand is doing." And your secret giving will be openly rewarded by the Father. (We will explore the relationship between giving and rewards in the next chapter.)

3.15. Conclusion

I think you see that giving under grace is not like giving under the law. Judging from these broad principles, I hope you see how much freedom there is under grace-giving.

Giving is like salvation.

We freely receive Jesus as our Savior. We receive the work He did on the cross and in His resurrection for ourselves. We receive the Holy Spirit and God's gifts of forgiveness, righteousness, and eternal life. The entire package is a gift, given to us by grace. We received all that freely, and we are called to give to others just as freely. Giving is a matter of the heart, not the law. There are no threats of the kind we find in the Mosaic Law or in Malachi 3.

However, we also saw that believers can gain or lose material and spiritual benefits based on their giving (e.g., the law of sowing and reaping). One of the most important things one can gain or lose is eternal rewards. That is an important subject that I will touch on in this next chapter as we further explore the relationship between giving and the heart.

Endnotes

1. Michael A. Eaton, *The Branch Exposition of the Bible: A Preacher's Commentary of the New Testament* (Cumbria: Langham, 2020), 631.

FOUR

Giving and the Heart

4.1. Introduction

If you've ever traveled internationally, you probably had to walk through a "duty-free" shopping store, where luxury goods like jewelry, whiskey, and chocolates were sold free of import taxes. You might have even walked through one of the stories owned by Duty Free Shoppers (DFS), co-founded by Charles Feeney in 1960. Over time, the company grew to have hundreds of millions of dollars in sales. By 1996, it was sold for over a billion dollars, making Feeney a very wealthy man.

Or, it almost did.

It turned out that Feeney did not own any shares in DFS. Not anymore. Years earlier, he had started Atlantic Philanthropies and secretly transferred all of his shares to it. When DFS was sold, the philanthropy got all the money, and through careful investing, it grew into billions of dollars. For the rest of his life, Feeney slowly, secretly, and anonymously gave away the entire fortune. It is estimated that Feeney gave away over $8 billion dollars. He paid for the construction of over a thousand buildings on five continents, and not a single one bears his name.

Just as striking, in his personal life, Feeney was extremely frugal. He never owned a car or a home. He flew coach and carried his reading materials in a plastic bag.

Whatever else you might say about him, Feeney clearly had a very different attitude towards money than most people in the world.

The same should be true of grace-believers.

We have looked at several grace-giving principles that make it very different from the popular teaching about tithing. The overarching truth is that, under grace, you can give *however much you purpose in your heart*. But that raises the crucial question: what's in your heart? Does it have the right priorities? Is it in the right place? If your heart is full of sin, greed, and covetousness, your giving will suffer. If you want to excel at grace-giving, you need to dig deeper into matters of the heart. And Jesus' teaching about giving does just that.

4.2. Where Your Heart Is

Sin has a way of trapping you before you realize it. F. Scott Fitzgerald famously said, "First you take a drink, then the drink takes a drink, then the drink takes you." In other words, the occasional sin can escalate into a persistent habit, which then festers into an addiction.

Greed is no exception.

Jesus knew how alluring and addictive money could be. Whenever your heart is addicted to something, you will think about it obsessively. Your dreams, plans, and goals will center around getting more of it, and the more you get, the more you will want. Jesus knew that money could capture our interests like few other things, which then creates a problem for discipleship. As the Lord warned:

> **"Don't store up for yourselves treasures on earth, where moth and rust destroy and where thieves break in and steal. But store up for yourselves treasures in heaven, where neither moth nor rust destroys, and where thieves don't break in and steal.** *For where your treasure is, there your heart will be also"* (Matthew 6:19-21, emphasis added).

In this passage, Jesus taught His disciples to change their mindsets—their heart attitudes—about money. He assumes our hearts will always be focused on treasure somewhere. The only question is, where? Will your heart be focused on treasure on earth or in heaven?

Notice that desiring treasures is not intrinsically wrong. The Lord is not against savings and investments per se, so long as it is heavenly.

Of course, you will be tempted to focus on building up earthly wealth. You need to fight that temptation. But how? One way is to change your thinking about how to value earthly wealth. In this passage, Jesus gives us several reasons for thinking we have overvalued earthly treasure.

First, earthly treasure can be *destroyed*. Wealth is not something you can depend upon. For example, three weeks ago, I was vacationing at a friend's cabin in Ruidoso, New Mexico, and I thought about how wonderful it would be to live there, or to have a vacation home there. I thought the owner was so lucky. And then, a week later, the cabin burned in a fire that devastated the entire village, destroying hundreds of homes and buildings. It had burned to the foundations.

Second, you can *lose* your treasure. It is estimated that the ocean floors are littered with billions of dollars' worth of treasure. More recently, a British man accidentally threw out a hard drive with over $270 million of Bitcoin. You are not guaranteed to have it forever.

Third, and even more commonly, earthly treasure can be *stolen*. Thieves can rob you, con men can swindle you, or the government can devalue the currency and therefore your savings. So far, I have lived through three recessions that destroyed the finances of untold numbers of people. No earthly treasure is safe from theft.

Each of Jesus' reasons should help change your attitude about finances. When you keep those considerations in mind, you will not value earthly treasure so highly.

By contrast, Jesus challenges us to think more deeply about the importance of investing in heavenly treasure which evidently lasts forever, and cannot be destroyed, lost, or stolen. Although the Lord doesn't clearly explain what the treasure is, and commentators disagree about how literally to take it, the Lord is communicating that heavenly treasure is far more desirable than anything we could accumulate on earth. You may not fully understand what that means, but if you have trusted the Lord with your salvation, you should also trust Him in this: *heavenly treasure is better than earthly treasure*. In other words, disciples should train their hearts to take an eternal perspective on treasure.

What can you do if you struggle with the sin of greed and find your mind filled with tempting thoughts of hoarding earthly treasure? It isn't enough to say "No" to those temptations. You need to fight them by building up the corresponding virtue. The more you have the virtue, the less tempting the sin will be.

For example, replace your old thoughts about earthly wealth with thoughts about gaining heavenly treasure or rewards. When you become convinced the latter are more valuable than the former, your heart will not be so tempted by them.

4.3. Serving God or Mammon

In his famous work, *Democracy in America*, Alexis de Tocqueville observed that Americans are especially concerned with earthly treasure:

> "I know of no country, indeed, where the love of money has taken stronger hold on the affections of men, and where a profounder contempt is expressed for the theory of the permanent equality of property. But wealth circulates with inconceivable rapidity, and experience shows that it is rare to find two succeeding generations in the full enjoyment of it."[1]

The heart seems forced to choose between earthly and heavenly treasures. Elsewhere, Jesus confirmed that money is a binary heart issue that rises to the level of idolatry:

> **"No one can serve two masters, since either he will hate one and love the other, or he will be devoted to one and despise the other. You cannot serve both God and money"** (Matthew 6:24).

When it comes to God and money, you probably want to have your cake and eat it, too. You may *think* you can compromise and find a way of loving both in a healthy way, but according to Jesus, that's impossible. You can't balance your loyalties between God and money. The choice is always binary. You'll either love God and hate money or love money and hate God. It's always one or the other.

Obviously, Christians should be dedicated to God alone. We're commanded to love God with *all* our hearts, minds, souls, and strength—which excludes loving money.

If your heart is ensnared by the almighty dollar, and mammon is your idol, that will affect your giving. After all, you probably won't want to give away the thing that you serve and prize above all else. Thus, to be a good giver, you must choose to serve God over mammon. And when you do, you can begin to see money for what it is—a tool to be used in Christian service.

When God is your master, money will be your servant.

4.4. Concern with Money Can Make You Unfruitful

An idolatrous focus on money will obviously impact your walk of faith for the worse. But Jesus also warned about less obvious ways in which having the wrong perspective on earthly treasure can hinder discipleship.

In the Parable of the Four Soils, a sower casts seed in a field. Some seed fell on thorny ground, and while a plant still grew, it never became fruitful. There was a tomato plant, but no tomatoes. Why not? Jesus explains:

> "Now the one sown among the thorns—this is one who hears the word, but the worries of this age and the deceitfulness of wealth choke the word, and it becomes unfruitful" (Matthew 13:22).

Jesus says the thorns represent *worries* and *the deceitfulness of wealth*. Both can stop you from being fruitful.

What are the worries of this age? They certainly include worrying about money, and everything related to it—e.g., paying for insurance, mortgage, and fixing your car. If your heart is set on your investment accounts, and you know how unstable the economy is, you'll constantly be thinking about them and so preoccupied with maintaining or gaining even more wealth. You'll put off serving the Lord to seek after mammon.

How is wealth deceitful? One way is that it promises earthly security and power when the reality is that it can be destroyed, lost, or stolen in a heartbeat. It promises comforts it cannot deliver on, especially in light of eternity.

Don't let the thorns of worry and wealth choke your fruitfulness.

4.5. Lay Up Treasure by Seeking the Kingdom

Instead of focusing your life on acquiring earthly treasure, Jesus calls you to seek something better. The Lord said:

> "But seek his kingdom, and these things will be provided for you. Don't be afraid, little flock, because your Father delights to give you the kingdom. Sell your possessions and give to the poor. Make money-bags for yourselves that won't grow old, an inexhaustible treasure in heaven, where no thief comes near and no moth destroys. For where your treasure is, there your heart will be also" (Luke 12:31-34).

Here again, Jesus encourages disciples to seek heavenly treasure.

Over the years, I've met Christians who are skeptical about that motivation. They think we should only serve God disinterestedly without being motivated by eternal rewards. They consider rewards to be selfish. While I understand that criticism, I think it's a mistake.

Jesus told us to seek the kingdom and to make "money bags" that "won't grow old." He urged us to store up "an inexhaustible treasure in heaven." That's not a motivation Jesus discourages or calls sinful, *but something He expects us to value and prioritize*. Whatever that treasure represents, we should value it more than earthly treasure. If someone thinks that's selfish, they should repent and bring their standards in line with Jesus' teaching. The Lord wants you to desire heavenly treasure.

Seeking the kingdom is not *selfish* so much as *self-interested*. It is a godly self-interest that is encouraged by Jesus Himself.

4.6. Greed Is Foolish

Throughout His ministry, people asked Jesus about money. The topic seems to have come up often. For example, one day, a man asked Jesus for help with his inheritance:

> Someone from the crowd said to him, "Teacher, tell my brother to divide the inheritance with me."
> "Friend," he said to him, "who appointed me a judge or arbitrator over you?" He then told them, "*Watch out and be on guard* against all greed, because one's life is not in the abundance of his possessions" (Luke 12:13-15, emphasis added).

This man's parents had died and left an inheritance to him and his brother. But they were quarreling over who got what. When one of the brothers asked Jesus to settle the matter, rather than get dragged into acting as their arbitrator, Jesus discerned a deeper problem: *greed*.

Sometimes, a perfectly legal request can be motivated by a hidden sin, making it sinful to do. In this case, Jesus discerned that the brother was asking for help out of *greed*. It is safe to say that we have all acted out of greed. How should we respond to that kind of temptation? Jesus says we should "watch out" and "be on guard." Indeed, those became the two watchwords of Christian spirituality for centuries.

To *watch out* (*horáō*) literally refers to seeing with your eyes, but came to mean being spiritually discerning. Pay close attention and watch out for the temptations and thoughts that will come to you, identifying them for what they are, and being sure to reject them.

To *guard* (*phylássō*) is to have uninterrupted vigilance. In other words, we guard our thoughts and motivations, always looking to discern the evil suggestions that come our way.

The fact is being greedy is foolish and short-sighted. To illustrate what He meant, Jesus told this parable:

> "A rich man's land was very productive. He thought to himself, 'What should I do, since I don't have anywhere to store my crops? I will do this,' he said. 'I'll tear down my barns and build bigger ones and store all my grain and my goods there. Then I'll say to myself, "You have many goods stored up for many years. Take it easy; eat, drink, and enjoy yourself."'
>
> "But God said to him, 'You fool! This very night your life is demanded of you. And the things you have prepared—whose will they be?'
>
> "That's how it is with the one who stores up treasure for himself and is not rich toward God" (Luke 12:16-21).

The rich man spent his life hoarding goods, planning for a comfortable future he would never enjoy. After he died unexpectedly, his hard-earned wealth went to other people, making his life-long selfishness a waste.

Worse, the man died without being "rich toward God," meaning there was no treasure waiting for him in heaven!

What this parable shows is that greed is not only *sinful* it is also *irrational*. It prioritizes short-term comforts over eternal benefits. The spiritually mature mind recognizes that this world is passing away and prioritizes using money to serve God rather than one's own selfish desires.

4.7. Making Friends with Money

Jesus taught us another positive way to use our money. Although you shouldn't love it, be devoted to it, or serve it, money is helpful for ministry.

For example, Jesus told an odd parable known as the Parable of the Dishonest Manager. In that story, a wealthy man hears that his steward has mismanaged his estate and demands a financial audit. The steward knows that he's guilty and will lose his job, so he takes action to make sure he at least has a soft landing. He goes to the clients who owe his boss large sums of money, renegotiates their contracts, and reduces what they owe. We're not told why he does that, but we can imagine it was to make the debtors grateful to him so they would owe him a favor, such as giving him a place to live. When the rich man finds out what happened, he praises the steward for at least being shrewd. Here's Jesus' application:

> "And I tell you, make friends for yourselves by means of worldly wealth so that when it fails, they may welcome you into eternal dwellings. Whoever is faithful in very little is also faithful in much, and whoever is unrighteous in very little is also unrighteous in much. So if you have not been faithful with worldly wealth, who will trust you with what is genuine? And if you have not been faithful with what belongs to someone else, who will give you what is your own? No servant can serve two masters, since either he will hate one and love the other, or he will be devoted to one and despise the other. You cannot serve both God and money" (Luke 16:9-13).

Here are some lessons Jesus expects us to draw from the parable.

First, we should make friends with worldly wealth so they will welcome us into "eternal dwellings." What does that mean? The unjust steward evidently hoped that he'd be given hospitality by the debtors he had helped. By analogy, Jesus might mean you can use your wealth to win souls so those people will welcome you in eternity. Won't that be amazing?

Second, if you're faithful with worldly wealth now, you'll be trusted with "much" and "genuine" heavenly wealth later. If you use your earthly wealth in the service of the kingdom, it will impact your heavenly wealth later. In other words, you'll have greater eternal rewards.

Third, Jesus contrasts loyalty to God and loyalty to money. You can't serve both, and you can't love both. The heart's choice is always binary: love one and hate the other; serve one or serve the other.

The spiritual mature approach is to use money for the sake of the gospel, so as to make eternal friends for yourself.

4.8. Jesus Will Reward Your Works

We have mentioned the idea of heavenly treasure and rewards and what place those should have in a renewed attitude towards wealth, and it may be time to explain them a bit more.

Christians have long noted that the New Testament refers to eternal rewards. But generally speaking, the doctrine of rewards was not developed until after the Reformation. Once Paul's doctrine of justification by faith apart from works was recovered from centuries of works salvation tradition, and it became clear once again that salvation is a *gift* given through faith apart from works (cf. Gal 2:16; Eph 2:8-9), commentators could then see there was a Biblical distinction between salvation and rewards.

Unlike salvation, heavenly treasures are earned as *payment* for the *works* that you do for the Lord. If you believe in Jesus, you'll never come under judgment for your eternal destiny (that issue was settled the moment you believed in Him, cf. John 5:24). However, you will still appear before the Lord to have your life evaluated. That day will not be about proving your salvation, but about assessing your faithfulness. That's why Jesus spoke about storing up treasure in heaven. He was referring to rewards given on the basis of what we've done for Him. Since not all Christians are equally faithful, some lay up more treasure than others.

As an illustration, do you remember the story of the three little pigs? Each one built a house. The ones that used straw and sticks did it faster and had more time to play. But it took longer for the pig to build his house out of bricks. However, all that hard work paid off when a big bad wolf came to town and was able to blow down the first two cheaply houses but not the house of bricks. The fable taught children that taking the easy route might result in immediate gratification, but only hard work pays off in the long run.

Paul used a similar illustration to teach the Corinthians about rewards. He compared living the Christian life to building a house (i.e., the body of Christ):

> **For no one can lay any foundation other than what has been laid down. That foundation is Jesus Christ. If anyone builds on the foundation with gold, silver, costly stones, wood, hay, or straw, each one's work will become obvious. For the day will disclose it, because it will be revealed by fire; the fire will test the quality of each one's work. If anyone's work that he has built survives, he will receive a reward. If anyone's work is burned up, he will experience loss, but he himself will be saved—but only as through fire (1 Corinthians 3:11-15).**

Paul taught that, like the three little pigs, every Christian is building something with their life. The only question is, what kind of materials are you using? It makes a big difference whether you're building with gold or straw.

For context, in the ancient world, fires were a serious threat. They didn't have the firefighting systems that we have today. If one house caught fire, it could spread quickly until the whole city was in flames. Cheaply made houses were most at risk of being burned up.

Similarly, at the judgment seat of Christ, the Lord Jesus will evaluate all of your works, and you'll be rewarded according to what survives the fires of His judgments. Unfaithful believers will have their worthless works burned up like so much wood, hay, and stubble, and instead of being rewarded, they'll experience loss.

Meanwhile, faithful builders who use fire-resistant materials—the equivalent of gold, silver, and jewels—will be rewarded by God. Their experience in eternity will somehow differ from that of believers who wasted their lives. Some commentators interpret the nature of these rewards literally, while others understand them figuratively. Whoever is right, those rewards will make a difference to the experience of the faithful servant.

But notice Paul's last statement. Even if someone has lived such a worthless life that all their works are burned away, *he will still be saved*, though "as through fire." Again, under grace, salvation is given as a gift apart from the works you do. Since you can't earn it by being good, you can't lose it by being bad. The only issue in salvation is whether or not you believe, not how consistently you have put that faith into practice.

Let me add a final thought. Since the good works we do come from Christ living in us (John 15:5; Gal 2:20), and the Holy Spirit empowering us (Gal 5:22-23; Rom 8:9-11), even though the rewards are based on what we do, I think there's a large measure of grace in them, too.

4.9. Not a Salvation Issue

Unfortunately, throughout the centuries, Christians have often been taught that going to heaven or hell depends on what you do—including what you do with your wallet. Confusion about money and salvation can be traced to a misreading of a few key texts, including this warning to Timothy:

> But godliness with contentment is great gain. For we brought nothing into the world, and we can take nothing out. If we have food and clothing, we will be content with these. But those who want to be rich fall into temptation, a trap, and many foolish and harmful desires, which plunge people into ruin and destruction. For the love of money is a root of all kinds of evil, and by craving it, *some have wandered away from the faith*

and pierced themselves with many griefs (1 Timothy 6:6-10, emphasis added).

Paul warned that fixating on getting rich caused some Christians to *wander from the faith* and even *come to grief*. Did Paul mean you could *lose your salvation* if you mishandled your money? Historically, many Christians have interpreted Paul that way. But if salvation is by faith apart from works (and it is!), that couldn't happen. The moment you believed, you were born again, passed from death to life, and Jesus promised never to cast you out (John 6:37). However, an eternally secure person can still sin. He can develop the wrong heart attitude towards money, wander into error and immorality due to greed, and suffer the consequences.

Which consequences?

Money is no guarantee of happiness. Seven out of ten of the wealthiest men in the world are divorced. Like any sin, the love of money can lead to negative earthly consequences.

Generally speaking, the sin of greed *will make you miserable*. As Paul said, you'll be pierced with "grief," a Greek word meaning "intense anxiety, anguish, grief, emotional pain." The love of money is a harmful desire that, if acted upon, can ruin your earthly life. Think of all the harm caused to marriages, families, careers, and reputations by foolish get-rich-quick schemes.

It can also lead to dire spiritual consequences. As Paul said, you could "wander" from the faith. To use Jesus' language, love of riches can choke away your fruitfulness (Luke 8:14). And if you don't produce mature fruit, you won't be rewarded. And that will mean at least some "grief" at the judgment seat of Christ.

So, what is the right attitude to have towards money? Instead of loving it so much that you keep wanting more, Paul says to be content with what you have: "godliness with contentment is great gain." How is contentment *gain*? An old Amish proverb explains it well, "You are only poor when you want more than you have." That redefines what it means to be rich. If you become content with what you have, you've gained the wealth you didn't realize was already yours.

In sum, the love of money can lead to serious negative earthly and spiritual consequences, but not to a loss of salvation. You should take those dangers seriously, but without compromising the gospel.

4.10. Conclusion

Grace giving is based on the motivations of your heart. Hence, it's important to have the right heart attitude towards finances. Believers should be on guard against greed and the love of money. Instead of setting our hearts on earthly treasure, we should set them on heavenly treasure. Instead of being an idol we serve, it should be a tool we use to serve the Lord.

Endnotes

1. Alexis de Tocqueville, *Democracy in America*, trans. Henry Reeve (New York, NY : J. & H.G. Langle, 1841), 1:52.

FIVE

Trust God With Your Finances

5.1. Introduction

When I studied theology at the Free University of Amsterdam, several classmates were international students from the developing world. It was a blessing to study alongside brothers and sisters in Christ from such different backgrounds, several of whom came to my apartment for a weekly meal. A few students were pastors from Ghana, and I remember one of them inviting me to visit his country.

"You don't need another white missionary coming to Ghana," I said. "You already have plenty of preachers!"

"Oh no," he corrected me. "I did not mean you should come to Ghana *as a missionary*. I meant you should come to learn what it means *to live as a Christian*."

I was taken aback.

"Shawn, you will never know what it means to pray until you do not know where your next meal will come from, and must depend upon God for it in prayer."

His word hit home!

To be perfectly honest, his invitation scared me. Frankly, I didn't want to be in a situation where I was so poor that I didn't know where my next meal was coming from. And now that I have a family to support, I still don't!

I don't think God's ideal is for us to be poor and starving. The Lord normally provides for our daily bread through our vocations, such as having a regular job with a regular income. Thank God for those daily provisions.

However, I've learned—and I'm still learning—that life is so filled with uncertainties that even if you're not worrying about your next meal, you can still worry about your finances in general. Hence, in this chapter, I want to address one incredibly unhealthy heart attitude many of us suffer from: *worry about finances*.

5.2. The Sin of Anxiety

Most of us have been taught to worry about money. I know I have. Day after day, the news is filled with politicians and pundits warning about the mountain of national debt, our unfunded liabilities, the impending collapse of social security, and the precariousness of the economy. We worry about our jobs, homes, retirement funds, and paying the mounting bills. I've already lived through several recessions and market crashes that ruined people's finances, and have talked to numerous people struggling in retirement.

Society is filled with voices telling us to worry about money. Hence, some people give less than they could, and hoard earthly treasures, not out of *greed* but due to *anxiety* over not having enough for tomorrow or their senior years.

If that's your struggle, consider what Jesus taught about worrying:

> "Therefore I tell you: *Don't worry about your life*, what you will eat or what you will drink; or about your body, what you will wear. Isn't life more than food and the body more than clothing? Consider the birds of the sky: They don't sow or reap or gather into barns, yet your heavenly Father feeds them. Aren't you worth more than they? Can any of you add one moment to his life span by worrying? And why do you worry about clothes? Observe how the wildflowers of the field grow: They don't labor or spin thread. Yet I tell you that not even Solomon in all his splendor was adorned like one of these. If that's how God clothes the grass of the field, which is here today and thrown into the furnace tomorrow, won't he do much more for you—you of little faith? So don't worry, saying, 'What will we eat?' or 'What will we drink?' or 'What will we wear?' For the Gentiles eagerly seek all these things, and your heavenly Father knows that you need them. But seek first the kingdom of God and his righteousness, and all these things will be provided for you. *Therefore don't worry*

about tomorrow, because tomorrow will worry about itself. Each day has enough trouble of its own" (Matthew 6:25-34, emphasis added).

Let me first point out that "Don't worry" is a *command*. Jesus forbade us from doing it, making anxiety *a sin*. Worrying about tomorrow is not morally innocent but a serious spiritual issue. You don't want to break this command and sin, do you? Then don't worry. This directive from Jesus gives us a clear path to follow, guiding us away from worry and towards faith.

Of course, that's easier said than done. You can't simply choose to stop sinning and put your mind in neutral. Believe me, I've tried! To overcome worry, you must do more than "Stop!" You need to change your old mindset and adopt new beliefs and perspectives to help you move from doubting God to trusting Him with your finances. In other words, you must replace your vice with virtue and unbelief with belief.

In Matthew 6:25-34, Jesus does more than give you the negative command to stop sinning but gives several positive reasons that explain why worrying is not the right attitude to take. In other words, the Lord disputes the false beliefs that might lead you to worry about tomorrow and encourages us to adopt true beliefs that will lead to peace.

First, you might worry about food and clothing because you think nothing is more important than those things. But is that true? As Jesus asks:

> "Isn't life more than food and the body more than clothing?"

The answer to this rhetorical question is *yes*, life is much more than food and clothing. Even if you lacked food or clothing now, what is that compared to the promise that believers shall live forever? (cf. John 11:25-26). But even in this life, it is more important to love our neighbors and serve God than to dress in fancy clothes and gorge ourselves on delicacies. Our lives are far more than earthly food and clothing, so why worry about them?

Second, you might worry because you don't think your life matters much to God. You might believe that God is ignorant or indifferent to your life below. You might think He's left you you on your own. If that's how you think, then Jesus says:

> "Consider the birds of the sky: They don't sow or reap or gather into barns, yet your heavenly Father feeds them. Aren't you worth more than they?" (v 26).

In other words, you shouldn't worry about life because you're more valuable to God than the birds. Since He takes care of them, He'll certainly take care of you.

Third, you might think that being anxious (you might call it being careful or prudent!) will help extend your life. If so, Jesus asks:

> **"Can any of you add one moment to his life span by worrying?" (v 27).**

The answer to His rhetorical question is "No." Worrying will not make you live longer. It doesn't improve any situation. On the contrary, we know that an anxiety-prone personality leads to many health problems and a shorter lifespan. Worrying will not add one second to your life, but it can take years away.

Fourth, you might worry because you lack faith in God's provisions. Maybe you don't believe that God provides for us every day. You might think your personal needs are too small for God to notice, let alone make a priority. You don't see what place you might have in God's plans. In that case, Jesus says:

> "And why do you worry about clothes? Observe how the wildflowers of the field grow: They don't labor or spin thread. Yet I tell you that not even Solomon in all his splendor was adorned like one of these. If that's how God clothes the grass of the field, which is here today and thrown into the furnace tomorrow, won't he do much more for you—you of little faith?" (vv 28-30).

Christians aren't Deists, and God isn't an absentee landlord. In other words, He didn't create the world only to be uninvolved in its existence. On the contrary, He exercises providential care over all things, right down to the wild grasses we casually trample underfoot without noticing. If God cares enough about the fields to clothe them with beautiful wildflowers, He will surely clothe you.

Fifth, you might worry because you don't think God knows what you need. Or maybe you don't believe He has the time to consider what you need to live. In which case, Jesus says:

> "So don't worry, saying, 'What will we eat?' or 'What will we drink?' or 'What will we wear?' For the Gentiles eagerly seek all these things, and your heavenly Father knows that you need them" (vv 31-32).

The Father knows. When you worry about those things, you act like a Gentile who has no God to provide for him. Instead of thinking that you're all on your own, trust your Father to care about you, to know what's best for you, and to provide.

Sixth, you might worry because your priorities are wrong. For example, you might be focused on building your own personal empire. If so:

> "But seek first the kingdom of God and his righteousness, and all these things will be provided for you" (v 33).

If you change your priorities and focus on seeking God's kingdom, Jesus promises you will be provided for. The very things you're prone to worry about will be provided by not worrying about them.

Seventh, you might think you're incapable of not worrying. Asking you to stop cold turkey may be asking too much. If so, here's a more manageable expectation:

> "Therefore don't worry about tomorrow, because tomorrow will worry about itself. Each day has enough trouble of its own" (v 34).

If you can't stop worrying all at once, at least stop worrying about tomorrow. If you must worry, turn your attention to today's troubles. That's not as comforting as the other reasons that Jesus gives, but it is realistic. Take life one day at a time.

Slowly changing your thinking patterns and perspectives, and taking a more informed view of how much God cares for you and values your life, can help you stop being anxious about finances.

5.3. God Is a Good Father

As we saw, several of Jesus' arguments revolve around changing your beliefs about the Lord's good character. That points to a source of worry: we're confused about how good God truly is.

We know God is powerful, but we're not sure how He'll use that power towards us because we're not sure that He's good. Clearly, Jesus prioritized replacing worry with better thoughts about God's goodness. To stop worrying about finances, God's goodness must be stamped on your heart.

Why can that be so hard to believe?

It's sad to say that not every father is good. Many people grow up with cruel and loveless fathers who have hurt or neglected them and their families. Children raised in loveless and abusive homes often grow up with trust issues, are dominated by the fear of failure, feel isolated, and generally don't prosper as much or as easily as children who grow up in a secure and loving environment.

The same insights apply to Christian discipleship.

If you do not believe that God is good but wonder if He will be cruel and neglectful towards you, that will negatively impact your discipleship. For example, confusion about God's good character will lead to fear over finances. But knowing that God is your loving Father will make all the difference in how you flourish. Look at what Jesus taught about the Father's goodness:

> **"Who among you, if his son asks him for bread, will give him a stone? Or if he asks for a fish, will give him a snake? If you then, who are evil, know how to give good gifts to your children, how much more will your Father in heaven give good things to those who ask him"** (Matthew 7:9-11).

What kind of Father is God?

Jesus argues from the lesser to the greater. If a decent Jewish father would never give his hungry son a deadly snake to eat, then how much more will God give good things to His children? Is God not as good as an earthly father? Unthinkable! God is much better, which means you can trust Him to be the source of all the good things you need.

Paul made a similar point to the Philippians.

5.4. God Is Your Supply

Who are you depending on for what you have? If you depend upon yourself and realize how undependable you are, then you'll worry. You'll also probably be more reluctant to give. If you're anxious that God will leave you high and dry if you give your money away, you probably won't give away very much.

If that's your fear, are there any promises of God that can help build faith in that area?

We saw how Jesus taught that God is a good Father who gives good things to His children. Along the same lines, here is what Paul told the Philippians:

> **And you Philippians know that in the early days of the gospel, when I left Macedonia, no church shared with me in the matter of giving and receiving except you alone. For even in Thessalonica you sent gifts for my need several times. Not that**

I seek the gift, but I seek the profit that is increasing to your account. But I have received everything in full, and I have an abundance. I am fully supplied, having received from Epaphroditus what you provided—a fragrant offering, an acceptable sacrifice, pleasing to God. *And my God will supply all your needs according to his riches in glory in Christ Jesus* (Philippians 4:15-19, emphasis added).

The Philippians had financially supported Paul's ministry on several occasions. At times, they were the only church that supported him ("no church shared with me...except you alone"). And in light of that giving, Paul knew that God would supply "all their needs according to his riches in glory in Christ Jesus." That was a promise to the Philippians, but I believe it illustrates a principle that applies to all believers (one we also saw in Christ's teaching about seeking first the kingdom). Your loving Father will supply what you need. As William MacDonald said, "this is a specific promise that those who are faithful and devoted in their giving to Christ will never suffer lack."[1] Or as Gundry says, "Since God is well-pleased with the Philippians' gifts, he'll 'fill all [their] need,' which means first and foremost (if not exclusively) that he'll supply all their financial need."[2] This is part of the larger principle of sowing and reaping (cf. Prov 11:24; Luke 6:38; Galatians 6:6-8; 2 Corinthians 9:6). God will provide.

This passage also illustrates that God supplies your needs *through other people*. How did Paul "have an abundance"? God didn't create it out of nothing but provided it through the Philippians.

God uses means, but He's your ultimate supply.

What difference should that make to you?

Think of all the different things your heart may depend upon to be your supply.

Imagine if you believed your *job* was your supply. Imagine you trusted your employer to pay you, provide medical benefits, and give you a good retirement. And then imagine that your company suddenly closed or they fired you. How would you react? You would probably become anxious, angry, depressed, or feel like your whole life was falling apart. Why? Because you were depending on your employer, and they failed you.

But what would happen if you lost your job while you trusted God to be your supply and believed your good Father knew all about what happened and what you needed? In that case, your perspective would be different, wouldn't it? You would still have inner peace because it never depended on your circumstances but on God's promise. So you would keep trusting God to continue supplying all your needs—only now, the Lord would use some other channel to do it. Having that perspective will make such a powerful impact on your life.

Do you also see how having that kind of restful attitude in God's provisions would make a difference to your giving? Under grace, you're supposed to give freely, out of a cheerful heart, according to whatever you have purposed to give. But if you don't trust God to be your supply, your heart might be fearful of not having enough, and you might not give at all. If that's your attitude, I'm not condemning you, and God doesn't condemn you either (because there's no condemnation in Christ, cf. Romans 8:1). God doesn't want you to give out of guilt, but cheerfully, trusting Him completely.

Now that you know His promise to supply your needs, are you willing to change your perspective, trust Him, step out in faith, and give?

5.5. Trust the Lord

Born-again people are meant to live the same way they were born again—*by faith*. That includes having faith in God for your finances.

Let me end this chapter with a proverb that was given to Israel:

> *Trust in the Lord with all your heart,*
> and do not rely on your own understanding;
> in all your ways know him,
> and he will make your paths straight.
> Don't be wise in your own eyes;
> fear the Lord and turn away from evil.
> This will be healing for your body
> and strengthening for your bones.
> *Honor the Lord with your possessions*
> *and with the first produce of your entire harvest;*
> *then your barns will be completely filled,*
> *and your vats will overflow with new wine* (Proverbs 3:5-10, emphasis added).

If you trust God with all your heart, that will include all those heart attitudes and thoughts about money.

Honor the Lord with your possessions, such as the "first produce of your entire harvest." In modern terms, that is like giving when you first get paid. That is significant because you're giving without knowing how the rest of the harvest, or the rest of your month, will pan out. Frankly, you don't know if you'll have enough money and food to last the month. Anything can happen.

Given that uncertainty, an atheist might urge you to save as much of your earnings as possible since you don't know the future. Maybe there will be a drought, fire, or hurricane that wipes out your crops and empties your bank account. Or perhaps you'll lose your job, have an unexpected medical emergency, or have a serious car repair. The future—your immediate future—is uncertain.

So when you give from your first harvest, without knowing if you'll have enough to last, you're saying you trust in God to provide for you the rest of the way. You're not hedging your bets or keeping anything back in case God fails to come through. You're walking by faith.

Giving your stuff away might not make worldly sense, but it makes spiritual sense because giving trains your faith to trust in God.

A grace-giving attitude says, "I don't know what the future holds, but I know who holds the future, and I trust the Lord to provide."

5.6. Conclusion

Many worldly reasons can prevent you from becoming a generous and cheerful grace-giver. Those mental attitudes should be disputed and replaced with Biblical truths. Mix your faith with Biblical teaching about God's good character and His promises to provide. As you do, your attitudes towards giving should change as you learn to give as generously as the Heavenly Father gives to you.

Endnotes

1. William MacDonald, *Believer's Bible Commentary*, ed. Art Farstad (Dallas, TX: Thomas Nelson, 1995), 1981.
2. Robert H. Gundry, *Commentary on the New Testament* (Peabody, MA: Hendrickson, 2010), 796.

Conclusion

Do Christians have to give ten percent of their income to the church or be cursed by God?

I hope this discussion has shown that the answer is a clear *no*. There are at least two key reasons why this teaching is problematic:

1. *Tithing is a Myth*. The Mosaic Law never required Israelites to tithe their income. Instead, it prescribed three tithes involving agricultural products—like crops and animals—intended to support priests, the poor, and various feasts. When these tithes were combined with other obligatory offerings, Israelites gave more than ten percent. So, the idea of tithing as a fixed income-based rule does not accurately reflect the Mosaic practice. The way that tithing is popularly taught is simply a myth.

2. *Christians Are Under Grace, Not Law*. Even if the Mosaic Law did require tithing, it wouldn't apply to believers in Christ anyway. Under grace, the law is no longer the standard for giving. Grace gives believers the freedom to give as they are led by the Spirit. The New Testament encourages free will offerings based on the principles of generosity, not legalistic mandates.

New Testament giving all comes down to grace. Grace transforms both salvation and discipleship, including giving. God's one-way love, demonstrated through the gift of His Son, reflects this grace. Ephesians 2:8-9 and Titus 3:5 affirm that salvation is a gift, given apart from our works, through faith. The same grace that saved you should shape your giving, motivating you to give freely, joyfully, and generously. Grace, not law, is what promotes godliness.

Where does that leave tithing?

You're free to tithe if you feel led by the Spirit to do so, but don't impose that as a rule on yourself or others. Don't make the mistake of thinking that's what God requires of everyone, and don't judge others for giving differently. Turning a personal decision to tithe into a new law would undermine the beauty of grace and turn giving into legalism.

Remember, grace-giving is about empowerment and encouragement, not fear and guilt. Grace-giving is not about fulfilling a legal requirement but about responding to the love and grace Jesus has shown us.

Jesus gave us salvation freely. Let His giving inspire your own. And the more that generosity flows from your heart, the more the joy of giving will flow in.

Discussion Questions

Introduction
1. In your experience, how have you seen tithing in churches? How has it affected your view on giving?
2. What do you think about tithing messages linked to blessings or curses, as in Malachi 3? How do these feelings influence your approach to giving?
3. The document suggests that tithing is a "myth" when applied to Christian giving. How does this change your views on financial obligations to the church?
4. What does it mean that Christians are called to give under grace, not law? How does this concept of grace change your perspective on generosity and giving?
5. The author contrasts fear-based giving with grace-based giving. What differences do you see between the two? How might grace-based giving inspire joy and freedom in your life?
6. How do you interpret the idea that "grace, not law, promotes godliness"? How can this principle affect your giving and your discipleship?
7. The document says that turning personal choices about giving into universal laws can undermine grace. How can churches encourage generosity without creating legalistic expectations?
8. How does knowing the context of Malachi 3 change your view on tithing and today's expected church donations?

9. The document emphasizes that Jesus gave His life freely for us. How does this example inspire or shape your attitude toward giving freely to others?

Chapter 1: The Myth of Tithing

1. How has the teaching of tithing shaped your view of giving in the church? Does this chapter challenge or affirm what you've been taught?
2. The chapter says the Mosaic Law had multiple tithes on farm products, not income. How does this change your view of "giving" in the Bible?
3. What do you think of the idea that tithing is a myth? Consider the agricultural requirements in Leviticus and Deuteronomy.
4. The author notes that popular teachings on tithing often misinterpret the Bible and oversimplify it. How important is it for modern Christians to study the context of these teachings for themselves?
5. The chapter explains that the Israelites gave tithes for various purposes, including supporting the Levites and the poor. How can churches today better reflect the purpose of these ancient practices?
6. After reading about the Festival Tithe and its focus on sharing, how should we emphasize joy and community in our giving?
7. The document says preachers often cite Abraham's giving a tenth of his battle spoils as a precedent for tithing. How does understanding the context of this one-time event affect your view of using Abraham as an example of regular tithing?
8. The chapter suggests Christians are not under the Mosaic Law. How should grace giving be incorporated into a modern believer's finances and spirituality?
9. How can churches shift from a law-based to a grace-centered model of giving? What challenges might arise in making this shift?
10. The chapter concludes by calling tithing a myth and raises the question of why many preachers still insist on it. How do you think tradition influences biblical interpretation and teaching within the church?

Chapter 2: Christians Are Not Under Law

1. How do you feel about the statement that Christians are not

under the Mosaic Law but under grace? How does this influence your understanding of faith?
2. What do you think about the pastor's claim in the opening story that "not paying tithes" leads to eternal condemnation?
3. How do the teachings of grace and law conflict when it comes to understanding salvation and giving in the modern church?
4. How has legalism, as described in this chapter, influenced your spiritual journey? Can you share any personal experiences of this?
5. What does it mean to live "under grace" in your day-to-day walk with Christ, and how does it change how you approach giving?
6. The chapter speaks about how the law produces wrath. How do you reconcile this with the gospel of grace and Christ's sacrifice?
7. How do you think legalistic teachings about tithing can distort the gospel message?
8. The chapter states that our salvation does not depend on works, including donations. How do you apply this truth to your current understanding of generosity?
9. How do you view the role of the law in teaching us about our need for Christ, as mentioned in the chapter?
10. How does knowing your freedom from the law affect your service and giving in your church community?

Chapter 3: Principles of Grace Giving

1. How do the examples of sacrificial giving, like the Macedonians, inspire your giving?
2. What does "give where you're fed" mean to you in the context of grace-based giving, and how can you apply this principle in your own life?
3. How do you determine how much to give when there is no fixed percentage, such as the 10% tithe?
4. What does it mean to "give according to your prosperity"? How do you assess your own prosperity when deciding how much to give?
5. How do you feel about giving to promote equality, as described by Paul in 2 Corinthians? How does this challenge or affirm your current giving habits?
6. What role does accountability play in ensuring that charitable giving is used wisely and effectively?

7. How can the principle of "sowing and reaping" motivate grace-based giving, and how do you avoid falling into the trap of prosperity theology?
8. The chapter encourages giving to inspire others. Can you share an example of how someone else's generosity has inspired you to give more freely?
9. How does the idea that grace-based giving is careful and thoughtful affect your approach to money and giving?
10. In what ways does grace-based giving allow for freedom, and how can this freedom be a source of joy rather than a burden?

Chapter 4: Giving and the Heart

1. How do you think your heart influences your approach to giving? What attitudes or beliefs must you address to align your heart with grace-based giving?
2. Jesus taught that "where your treasure is, there your heart will be also." How does this challenge you in evaluating your current financial priorities?
3. What steps can you take to shift your focus from storing up earthly treasures to storing up heavenly ones?
4. The chapter warns about the deceitfulness of wealth. How have you seen this play out in your own life or the lives of others?
5. How do you balance being responsible with money while avoiding the trap of making it an idol or source of worry?
6. How does the Parable of the Rich Fool challenge you regarding how you handle your resources and prepare for the future?
7. The chapter speaks about making friends with money to invest in eternity. How can you use your financial resources to bless others and make an eternal impact?
8. How does knowing that Jesus will reward our good works, including giving, affect your motivation to be generous?
9. What practical steps can you take to cultivate a heart that serves God over mammon (money)?
10. How does the teaching on heavenly rewards help you stay focused on long-term, kingdom-oriented giving?

Chapter 5: Trust God With Your Finances

1. How does the story about the Ghanaian pastor change your view on relying on God for daily needs?
2. Jesus taught us not to worry about tomorrow. How does this

teaching challenge or comfort you regarding your financial future?
3. How does society's focus on financial security fuel money anxiety? How can you escape that mindset?
4. How does knowing that God is a good Father who provides for your needs impact how you approach giving and trusting Him?
5. What does it mean for you to "seek first the kingdom of God," especially regarding how you manage your resources?
6. How does God's promise to meet your needs (Philippians 4:19) comfort you in tough times?
7. How can you replace worry with trust in God's provision, as Jesus encourages in Matthew 6:25-34?
8. The chapter speaks about God using others to supply your needs. How have you experienced God's provision through the generosity of others?
9. How does sowing and reaping affect your view of giving and God's provision?
10. How can you ease financial worries and trust God as your provider?

Subject Index

Apostles 37
Charity 12, 39
Covenant 7, 19, 28-31, 33-34, 43
Discipleship 18, 48, 50, 64, 69
Eternal life 20-22, 26, 45
Faith 20-27, 31, 42-43, 50, 54-57, 60-62, 64, 66-67, 70
Finances 3, 39, 49, 58-61, 63-64, 66
Forgiveness 21, 45
Free Grace 2
Free will 69
Giving 1-3, 5, 9-10, 12-14, 19, 23, 28, 30-31, 33-45, 47-48, 50, 53, 57, 64-67, 69-70
Gold 55-56
Gospel 18, 20-21, 23-25, 34, 37, 39, 41-42, 54, 57, 64
Grace 1-3, 17-18, 23, 26-28, 31, 33-37, 41-42, 44-45, 48, 56-57, 66, 69-70
Heaven 6-7, 17, 19-20, 44, 48, 51-53, 55-56, 64
Hell 56
Heresy 23
Holy Spirit 45, 56
Justification 24, 54
Kingdom of God 29, 60, 63
Money 9, 34-36, 38-39, 41, 47-48, 50-54, 56-58, 60, 64, 66-67
New Covenant 28, 30-31, 34, 43
New Testament 13, 27, 45, 54, 67, 69
Offerings 13, 16, 69
Old Testament 31
Prophecy 25, 29, 42
Propitiation 25
Resurrection 25, 28, 45
Righteousness 20-21, 23, 25-26, 30, 44-45, 60, 63
Salvation 17, 20-21, 23, 25-27, 45, 49, 54-57, 69-70
Scripture 2-3, 16

Sin 6, 20-21, 23-25, 29, 41, 48-49, 52, 57, 60-61
Support 12, 14, 34, 37, 41, 59, 69
Tithe 5, 10-12, 14-16, 18, 28, 31, 33, 69-70
Tithing 1-2, 7-11, 13, 15-17, 26, 28, 30-31, 41, 48, 69-70
Treasure 48-55, 58
Worship 35

Scripture Index

Genesis 1 .... 15, 42	Isaiah 53:5-6 25
Genesis 13 15	Ezekiel 36:25-27 29
Genesis 14:16 15	Malachi 3 .... 5-7, 30, 45
Genesis 14:20 15	Malachi 3:7-12 6
Genesis 28:10-22 16	Matthew 5:1 25
Exodus 13:2, 13....................... 13	Matthew 5:3 43
Exodus 30:13-16 13	Matthew 5:17 25
Exodus 35:20-29 13	Matthew 6:1 48
Leviticus 2.................... 10, 13-14	Matthew 6:2 .... 50, 61
Leviticus 7:16 13	Matthew 6:24 50
Leviticus 23:10-14 13	Matthew 12:3 21
Leviticus 25:1-7 14	Matthew 12:36 21
Leviticus 25:8-55 14	Matthew 13:2 51
Numbers 18:15-16 13	Matthew 13:22 51
Deuteronomy 15:7-11 14	Mark 10:1 6
Deuteronomy 27:26................. 19	Mark 10:18 6
Deuteronomy 28:15................. 19	Luke 6:3........................ 43-44, 65
Psalm 1 .... 19, 25	Luke 6:38 65
Psalm 14:1-3 19	Luke 8:1.................................. 57
Psalm 51:7, 12 29	Luke 8:14 57
Psalm 73:3-5, 12-14 20	Luke 12:1 52-53
Proverbs 11:24........................ 40	Luke 12:3 51
Proverbs 19:17........................ 37	Luke 22:2 30

Luke 22:20 30	Romans 6:14 18
John 1:1 .... 18, 25-26	Romans 7:2 24
John 1:2 25	Romans 7:4 28
John 1:12 26	Romans 7:6 28
John 1:14 25	Romans 7:9 41
John 1:29 25	Romans 7:23 24
John 2:2 25	Romans 8:1 66
John 3:1 .... 21, 26	Romans 9:3 27
John 3:3 22	Romans 9:30 27
John 3:18 21	1 Corinthians 3:1 55
John 3:36 22	1 Corinthians 16:2 35
John 5:2 .... 22, 55	2 Corinthians 8:1 37-39
John 5:24 55	2 Corinthians 9:1 42
John 6:3 57	2 Corinthians 9:6 .... 40, 65
John 6:37 57	2 Corinthians 9:8 41
John 11:2 61	Galatians 2:1 27
John 15:5 56	Galatians 2:16 27
Acts 13:3 21	Galatians 3:1 25
Acts 16:2 34	Galatians 3:2 24
Acts 16:20 34	Galatians 3:13 25
Acts 17:3 20	Galatians 3:24 24
Romans 1:1 20	Galatians 4:4 25
Romans 2:1 21	Galatians 6:6 34
Romans 2:13 21	1 Thessalonians 1:6 34
Romans 3:1 19	Titus 3:5 69
Romans 3:2 .... 21, 23, 26	Hebrews 7:4 15
Romans 3:20 23	James 1:2 42
Romans 3:28 26	1 Peter 2:2 25
Romans 4:1 .... 19, 26	1 Peter 2:24 25
Romans 4:5 26	1 John 2:2 25
Romans 4:15 19	Revelation 20:1 21
Romans 4:16 26	Revelation 20:12 21
Romans 5:1 26	
Romans 6:1 18	

Check Out These Books

- John Goodding, *Not So Famous Amos*
- John Goodding and Lucas Kitchen, *Evan Wants To Go To Heaven*
- Lucas Kitchen, *Eternal Clarity*
- Lucas Kitchen, *Eternal Life: Believe to Be Alive*
- Lucas Kitchen, *Eternal Rewards: It Will Pay to Obey*
- Lucas Kitchen, *For the Sake of the King*
- Lucas Kitchen, *In Pursuit of Fruit*
- Lucas Kitchen, *Missionary to Mars*
- Lucas Kitchen, *Naked Grace*
- Lucas Kitchen, *Salvation and Discipleship*
- Lucas Kitchen, *Things Above*
- Lucas Kitchen, *Thomas: Hero of the Faith*
- Shawn Lazar, *The Five Points of Free Grace*
- Shawn Lazar, *The Myth of Tithing and the Joy of Grace Giving*

Buy them and more at www.freegrace.in/shop

SHAWN LAZAR (BTh, McGill; MA, Free University, Amsterdam) was born and raised in Montreal, Canada. He and his wife Abby live with their three children in Denton, TX. He writes and edits for Free Grace International (www.freegrace.in). Listen to his podcast, *Chapter by Chapter with Shawn Lazar* on all the most popular platforms. He is the author of:

- *Beyond Doubt: How to Be Sure of Your Salvation*
- *Chosen to Serve: Why Divine Election Is to Service, Not to Eternal Life'*
- *One-Point Preaching: A Law and Gospel Model*
- *Scripturalism and the Senses: Reviving Gordon H. Clark's Apologetic*
- *It Takes God to Be a Man: The Spiritual Theology of Major Ian Thomas*
- *Free Grace Family Catechism*
- *The Five Points of Free Grace*

www.ingramcontent.com/pod-product-compliance
Lightning Source LLC
Chambersburg PA
CBHW060348050426
42449CB00011B/2874